A GIRL'S GUIDE TO BEING FEARLESS

How to Find Your Brave

Suzie Lavington and Andy Cope

CAPSTONE

This edition first published 2021

© 2021 by Suzie Lavington and Andy Cope

Registered office

John Wiley & Sons Ltd, The Atrium, Southern Gate, Chichester, West Sussex, PO19 8SQ, United Kingdom

For details of our global editorial offices, for customer services and for information about how to apply for permission to reuse the copyright material in this book please see our website at www.wiley.com.

Library of Congress Cataloging-in-Publication Data

Names: Lavington, Suzie, author. | Cope, Andrew, 1966- author.
Title: A girl's guide to being fearless : how to find your brave / Suzie
    Lavington and Andy Cope.
Description: Chichester, West Sussex, United Kingdom : Wiley, 2021. |
    Includes index.
Identifiers: LCCN 2020033401 (print) | LCCN 2020033402 (ebook) | ISBN
    9780857088574 (paperback) | ISBN 9780857088680 (adobe pdf) | ISBN
    9780857088611 (epub)
Subjects: LCSH: Girls—Psychology—Juvenile literature. | Courage—Juvenile
    literature. | Self-esteem in children—Juvenile literature.
Classification: LCC HQ777 .L378 2021 (print) | LCC HQ777 (ebook) | DDC
    155.43/3—dc23
LC record available at https://lccn.loc.gov/2020033401
LC ebook record available at https://lccn.loc.gov/2020033402

Cover Design: Wiley
Cover Image: Amy Bradley

Set in 10/14pt Frutiger LT Std by SPi Global, Chennai, India

Printed in the UK by Bell & Bain Ltd, Glasgow

10 9 8 7 6 5 4 3 2 1

A GIRL'S GUIDE TO BEING FEARLESS

For Amelie and Remy.
I suspect this book might do a better job of parenting you through your
teens than I will in real life. So when I disappoint, try zoning me out
and opening these pages instead. x
- Suzie

For Sof.
I've watched you grow from fearless girl to sassy young woman.
Thanks for making me so proud. x
- Andy

CONTENTS

Chapter 18.
HOW TO NEVER DO A DAY'S WORK IN YOUR LIFE

Page 179

Chapter 19.
THE GREATEST STORY EVER TOLD

Page 189

A GIRL'S GUIDE TO BEING FEARLESS

Tired of trying to cram her sparkly star-shaped self into society's beige square holes, she chose to embrace her ridiculous awesomeness and shine like the freaking supernova she was meant to be.

-Unknown

Chapter 1

A LETTER TO THE SISTERHOOD

DARLING READER,

Congratulations on an excellent choice of book. We hope you enjoy every last page, even the ones you find challenging. Which might include these first few. Sorry.

First up, a small confession: we've misled you with the title. Being 'Fearless' isn't actually a thing. You can't be a properly functioning human being and feel no fear at all. It's a perfectly normal – and sometimes useful – emotion. Love it or loathe it, fear will keep showing up in your life, to some degree or other, forever.

Our goal with this book isn't to rid you of it. Quite the opposite. We *want* you to feel fear. Often. We'll explain ourselves in Chapter 9, but basically it's a sure-fire sign that you're pushing yourself to be better. And that's something you should want to do every day. Not better than 'her' off the telly, or 'her' on Instagram, or even 'her' at school. But better than the version of yourself that you were yesterday.

Our goal, instead, is to help you acknowledge fear when it shows up. Shake its hand. Give it a front row ticket to watch you cracking on *in spite* of it. . . and occasionally glance in its direction to give it a cheeky wink, so it never forgets who's running the frickin' show.

So, yeah, we *want* you to feel fear. And while we're at it, there are a few other things we want for you, too.

From time to time in the years to come, we hope you'll be treated unfairly. Perhaps you'll miss an opportunity through no fault of your own or get blamed for someone else's mess. And we hope these things happen frequently enough that you'll come to know the value of justice. We hope you'll learn a bonus lesson when you're out the other side – how to shake it off and move onwards, with a beautiful smile on your beautiful face.

We hope that, at some point, your bestie lets you down. Sure, you'll feel awful but, fingers crossed, it'll teach you the importance of loyalty. And, sorry to say, but we also hope you'll feel lonely now and then. Not big bouts of loneliness, they're plain horrible, but long enough stretches for you to learn never to take friends and family for granted.

We also wish you bad luck – again, from time to time – so that you'll be conscious of the role of chance in life and understand that your success isn't always deserved... and that the failure of others isn't always deserved either. And when you lose, which you will (frequently), we hope some of your opponents gloat over their victory. It'll be during those times that you'll understand the importance of winning with grace.

We hope you'll be ignored so you know the importance of listening to others, and we hope you'll feel just enough pain to learn compassion.

We wish you illness, both minor and major. An occasional toothache, migraine or period pain will be enough to remind you to appreciate the fact that most of the time your body does a marvellous job of getting you around town. Please don't take this next sentence the wrong way, but we also wish you something more substantial; a recoverable health scare that truly knocks you for six. Once you've crawled yourself back to wellness, we're confident you'll have a refreshed attitude to the simple miracle of being alive.

Mentally, we wish you an occasional bout of something that robs you of your mojo – temporarily, of course. An episode of sadness can have rejuvenating properties. Learning to cope with your thoughts is one of life's biggest challenges, but luckily for you, that's what this book is all about.

At school, we hope there's at least one subject you hate, probably taught by a teacher you loathe. Time will surely drag and you'll struggle to see the point of being there. . . until later in life, when you attend boring management meetings chaired by incompetent bosses, and you'll realise those hateful lessons were excellent prep.

Career-wise, we hope you don't nail every job interview you sit through and that, on occasion, inferior colleagues get promoted ahead of your brilliant self. There'll be a lesson to take away. . . though we're not entirely sure what that one is. Temporary gnashing of teeth is okay, but contrary to popular belief, the best revenge isn't to let their tyres down. It's to truly shine at work and make your employer wonder how the hell they could have got it so wrong in the first place.

And if we could be granted two more wishes, we'd save the biggest till last.

Firstly, love. We sincerely hope you fall headlong into the stuff, and that one or two of those relationships come to an end. We hope it feels like your life has been torn apart. . . and that's good, because it basically will have been. And after weeks of sobbing, we hope you learn to move on. Stronger, with lessons learned, and a sharpened ability to find better, longer-lasting love. We truly hope your bad experiences don't stop you loving in the future. Rather, they make you better at loving. We hope you twig that moving on and living well really is the best revenge. Our hope (and it's a biggie) is that you realise that being nasty to someone who broke up with you might – just *might* – mean they were right about you all along.

Which brings us to bereavement. Once again, please take this next sentence in the manner in which it's intended: we hope that, on occasion, someone close to you passes away. Elderly great-grandparents might be easiest to cope with, but sometimes, beautiful girl, it's going to have to be closer than that. And it'll be gut-wrenchingly painful. We hope that you'll wrap yourself up in the love of those around you. And that, in time, you'll heal and move forward, holding them tightly in your heart and accepting that that's simply how the circle of life rolls around. One day, it'll be you who's gone and that gut-wrenching feeling will pass down to the next generation, as it has since humans were invented.

The point is that whether we wish these things or not, they're 100% going to happen. Every single one of them. Indeed, some will happen several times.

People may call these occasions 'tragedies' or 'plot twists'. We just call them 'the facts of life'.

Life isn't fair, but then, if you stop and think about it, nobody ever said it was. Try starting from the position that life isn't ever going to be fair and you'll feel your anxiety wash away.

Sure, some people seem to have more of it to contend with, but adversity is a consequence of being alive. And whether you benefit from it will depend upon your ability to see the message in the misfortune.

Oh, and one last thing: remember, there is one fact that often gets forgotten. It's this: life also has its ups. Loads of them. Don't forget to relish those.

So much love, Suze and Dr Andy

xx

Tell me, what is it that you plan to do with your one wild and precious life?

-Mary Oliver

Chapter 2

IN THE BEGINNING. . .

A true story.
About a toaster.

There are a lot of *in-one-ear-out-the-other-ear* books. I know, because I've read a few. Don't ask me what happens in them because I can't remember.

This isn't one of those.

I wrote *Girl's Guide* to be a kick-startin', cage-rattlin', thought-provokin', page-turnin', habit-formin', confidence-boostin', game-changin' kind of book.

I want the words to go in one ear and *hang around*. Sure, I want the book to delight you, but also to challenge you, maybe even irritate you. Because if I can provoke an emotion, you'll keep reading.

And if you keep reading, you'll learn heaps of stuff that you can apply to your life. . . and, in turn, make it bonkersly epic.

So here comes the million-dollar question: how do I begin? Because if I begin where all other books begin, *Girl's Guide* becomes just another one of those.

And that'll never do.

So strap yourself in. There's a massive point coming, but the best way to make it is via a slightly weird story.

A true story. About a toaster.

My toaster.

My *new* toaster.

I unpacked said toaster and placed it in pride of place next to my kettle. I noticed the new toaster came with an instruction manual; a weighty document, written in 14 languages. I skipped 13 of the languages and dived straight into the bit about how to make actual toast. And I quote:

1. Plug toaster in.
2. Turn the knob to the desired colour (your toast can come out white, brown or charcoal. Who knew?).
3. Place bread (bagel, muffin, crumpet, pop tart) into the slot.
4. Press the thingymajig down.
5. Wait. (Maybe get a knife and plate while you're waiting. Or check your phone.)
6. Bread will pop up. But it's changed its name. The bread from 90 seconds ago has been rebirthed as 'toast'.
7. Butter it (jam, marmalade, Nutella, or poached egg and avocado if you're posh).
8. Scoff it.
9. Repeat until tummy is full or school bus is pulling up outside.

So, there you have it. That's the official instruction manual for my new toaster.

Now, it just so happens that I've also got a brand-new daughter. After the rather surreal experience of a planned caesarean section (in which I was given a magical drug that numbed me from the chest down and a team of surgical marvels carried out what felt like the washing up in my stomach), she emerged, weighing in at 7 pounds 11 ounces. Once my elated husband had cut her cord, the midwife dabbed her down a bit, wrapped her in a blanket and placed her gently on my chest. There we were, mother and daughter. Neither of us looking our best. Me: anaesthetised to the eyeballs, nightie all skew-whiff. And newborn Remy: scrunched up like a raisin, covered in goo.

Our eyes met.

(Reminder: we BOTH LOOKED YUCK.)

And we fell in love. For ever and ever. Amen.

And as I lay there staring at my squidgy little newborn, it struck me that from this day forward, time would fly. In the blink of an eye, she'd say her first word ('mama', hopefully!) and take her first wobbly step. She'd go through the terrible twos. Then, before I'd know it, she'd be getting all dressed up in her school uniform and toddling off for her first day at primary school (and I'd definitely 'ugly cry' but try my hardest to hide it from her).

Then she'd end up in secondary school, with all the associated pressures of curriculum and relationships and boy/girlfriends. I knew that one day, in her teenage years, we'd have a slanging match in the kitchen. Remy would scream that she hated me, and I'd be terribly upset but wouldn't love her a fraction less.

I figured that, fingers crossed, one day she'd get a job, something she really enjoyed, and maybe even have kids of her own. And even if I reached the wrinkly old age of 100, and she'd be 65, I'd never stop being in awe of my 'little girl'. I'd help her through life's ups and downs, of which there would be many. Who knows, maybe she'd help me through a few of my own.

The very second she was handed to me, Remy became a lifetime commitment. And as I gazed lovingly at this tiny human, I realised that she was the most complex piece of kit I'd ever been given.

And yet there was no instruction manual.

So, my toaster, the simplest contraption in the world, comes with a comprehensive user manual, written in 14 languages. Yet my newborn daughter, the most complex thing I'll ever have to operate, comes with zilch.

I've written this piece because, guess what? It's how you arrived, too. A few years ago, you arrived in the world, blinking at the lights, gazing up at your mum, and she didn't have a clue. And now you're a teenager, she still doesn't. Ditto for your dad.

Your parents/carers/teachers are literally making it up as they go along. That means they'll make mistakes along the way. They'll get it wrong so many times. Always remember, you didn't come with a user manual. So when they mess up and press your wrong buttons, cut them some slack.

They're doing their best to operate the most complex piece of kit in the known universe – a teenage girl.

But here's the thing. Yes, your parents are making it up as they go along, but so are you! Life is the oldest game in town and yet it has the most complicated rules. In fact, 'LIFE' is the only game in the world where the objective is to learn the rules, understand them, and then be confident enough to bend a few.

Thank you for choosing to read *A Girl's Guide to Being Fearless*.

It might be the closest thing you'll ever get to an instruction manual. Shall we dive in?

FACT: People who shine from within don't need the spotlight

Chapter 3

TWO QUESTIONS, TWO TRUTHS AND A LIE

A WAKE-UP CALL:

Rise and shine, lady, your BEST life awaits!

What I didn't tell you in the previous chapter is that Remy has an older sister. As I write these words, my eldest daughter, Amelie, is three years old.

Amelie. Is. Awesome.

She carries herself around with what can only be described as a 'toddler swagger': chest puffed out, arms swinging confidently by her sides, chucking herself wholeheartedly into every single step. She's hugely proud of who she is and what she can do, and takes up her space without apology.

Now, if you've spent even the smallest amount of time in the company of a three-year-old, you might be familiar with their tendency to burst into song and/or dance, any time, anywhere, and for anyone. Amelie's no exception and I chuffin' well love her for it. And I'm not talking quaint little ditty paired with graceful balletic movement. I'm talking head thrown back, voice at full belt, limbs at full stretch while she hurls herself across the room in a shameless display of absolutely loving life. And I use 'shameless' in the very best sense of the word (we all desperately need to carry around less shame. . . more on that later).

And heaven help anyone who claps when she's 'not finished yet!' or forgets to clap when she clearly has. For the record, the end of every performance is signalled by an over-enthusiastic bow. . . a bow she'll keep taking until you've thrown precisely the right amount of applause and glory her way. She's rather partial to a standing ovation, is my Amelie.

She also LOVES her reflection. Every time she catches herself in the mirror, she beams. Then she'll strike a pose. Or twenty. I'm not kidding, that little cupcake could spend hours alone with any reflective surface, just. . . loving herself. Smiling at the image staring back at her. Sometimes even kissing it.

I know most little humans do this. If I really think back, I know I used to do it, too. And so did you!

The question is, then: when did I stop? When did I stop demanding standing ovations? When did I stop looking in the mirror and thinking, *'Oh wow, get a loada me! Look at what I can do! How blinkin' brilliant am I?'*

When, instead, did I start thinking, *'Well, wuddya look at the state of that!'*

'Look at the dark circles under my eyes!'

'Look how hideous my thighs look in these tights!'

'What in the name of sod has happened to my hair?'

'Zit alert! My life is over!'

'I hate my horrible teeth/nose/stomach/[insert any body part imaginable!]. What can I wear to cover that up?'

'I've got a massive day ahead of me today. . . what's the betting I'm gonna balls it up?'

It's incredible how we do this to ourselves, isn't it? Like some masochistic religion: every morning, we stand in front of our reflections, home in on the bits of our bodies we dislike, and promptly annihilate ourselves with a barrage of abuse.

When so many of us start our days like this, is it any wonder we sometimes feel like we're limping through them, mentally battered and bruised?

I mean, where in the name of fudge did our courageous little three-year-old selves go? The ones who loved the limelight? The kids who threw their arms wide and welcomed each new day?

If that's how we all started, when did we stop?

The answer, I guess, is that there was probably no single moment or event. It was a gradual drip, drip, drip over many years – of other people's nonsense getting inside our head. Friends, parents, teachers, siblings, film and TV.

Put that all together and you get 'culture' – the way things are – and to feel safe and secure you have an inbuilt desire to fit in. You become part of the nonsense.

But the brilliant news is that as a teen, you're old enough to read this book and young enough to change. And by 'change' I mean upgrade your thinking and habits.

Aside from perhaps a couple of inbuilt phobias, we're all born with just one emotion: love. We want to give it and we want to receive it. How brilliantly uncomplicated!

Newborn babies don't need therapy or counselling. We're born a blank slate with what Buddhists call our 'original face'. You're pure YOU. No hang-ups or embarrassment. You unashamedly pooped your nappy and let mum/dad wipe you down and stick a fresh one on. You didn't lie there, all embarrassed, while your poor old dad retched as he cleaned you up. You just wriggled and giggled and thought you were fabulous.

And when he was done, you did it again! *Cue more giggling.*

You had no beliefs or prejudices. Babies aren't racist or sexist. Babies can't even recognise themselves in a mirror. Aged nine months, when your mum showed you YOU in the mirror, you didn't think, *'Holy cow. I'm chuffin' bald! And why hasn't someone told me I've got baby food slapped all over my forehead? No way! Look at my forearms. . . they're fat! OMG. . . is that my belly? And get a load of these chubby cheeks. I'm half human, half hamster! I can't ever go out in public.'*

Nope. You just smiled and dribbled.

But as we get older, we start to develop a sense of self. We begin to understand that the person in the mirror is us. And that's great in primary school, but then something else kicks in when you reach double-digit age. We begin to get a sense of what other people think about us.

That small sentence has massive implications.

Up until that point, your child brain has thoughts but hasn't twigged that all the other brains have thoughts, too. Once that particular penny drops, you start to worry about what other people might be thinking *about* you. So instead of just going for it, you start to withdraw and be cautious. You stop jumping in puddles because, well, what would people think? You look around at everyone else in full make-up mode and do the same because *if I venture out with my natural face, what on earth will people think?*

The *drip, drip, drip* effect means the tap of gushing enthusiasm and joy of life gets gradually turned off. If you're not careful, the gush becomes a trickle. And if you look around at some of the adults in your life, their tap has been turned off completely.

My message to you is this: look around at the masses – the hordes of human beings who hibernate in a state of bog-standard, waking up briefly for a week's holiday, before returning to their slumbering averageness – AND DON'T EVER BECOME THAT!

Their inner adventurer is in sleep mode. *Deep* sleep mode.

Girl's Guide is a reminder – a wake-up call. Rise and shine, lady, your best life awaits!

But before we get into the proper nitty-gritty, I have to share two HUGE questions, two MASSIVE truths and a BIG FAT lie.

The first HUGE QUESTION is this: *what are you?*

Whatever name you go by, you are made up of 37 trillion cells that stick together to form 'you'. Each of those cells is a tiny dot of energy.

So you are energy. *Pure* energy.

General knowledge tells you that cells die and are regenerated. For example, the cells on your tongue live for a few hours before dying and being replaced by a fresh new taste bud. Red blood cells live for a few weeks, white blood cells a matter of days. Liver cells get a bit longer. Colon cells get a few months.

Yada yada, whatever.

My point is this: every cell in your body dies and is regenerated. The whole regeneration process takes about six months. Bottom line, in six months from now, you will be an entirely new human being. You will be a completely different 37,000,000,000,000 cells.

A completely new you.

So, HUGE QUESTION number 2 is this: *what kind of you do you want to be?*

Because MASSIVE TRUTH number 1 is that you can have a pulse but not be pulsating with life.

'Presenteeism' is a business word that's used to describe people who show up at work but go through the motions. They're logged on from 9.01 to 4.59, occupying a desk, sucking up oxygen and drinking bad coffee, but they're not really there. Not fully.

Except 'presenteeism' isn't just about work. It can also apply to school and life. Look around. There are a lot of people logged on, breathing, drinking bad coffee – but not many who are buzzing.

It's my belief that life is a short and precious gift. In the history of the universe, you live for such a brief flicker – isn't it worth making that pulse of yours race a bit? Isn't it worth putting a bit of effort into something a bit naughty, different, memorable, thrilling or adventurous? Or how about working at being more optimistic, hopeful, energetic, dynamic and positive?

But there's a line to be drawn somewhere, right? I agree. You can overdo it. There's an old English word – grinagog: someone who's so annoyingly happy that you want to punch them on the nose.

I'm absolutely NOT into that. If you're annoying people with your zest for life, you're doing it wrong. Rather, I want you to take them with you on your journey. I want you to be infectious. In a wonderfully uplifting way.

Which begs the question, *why are there not more of them?* The infectious ones? The wonderfully uplifting human beings. The genuinely sparkling people who energise and inspire. Why is it that you can count them on the fingers of one hand?

Plenty more on that later.

At this point, all you need to know is that the answer lies in human nature. We're social creatures. Pack animals. We're hardwired to fit into a team, tribe, clan, gang, family, community. . . we have an overwhelming desire to be part of something social. So, we look around at what everyone else is doing, and we copy. Because when we look, sound and behave like others, we belong. Humans crave a sense of belonging because it makes us feel safe.

Which is where it gets difficult. Safety is built into the human operating system. It's a basic need.

My argument is that playing safe is all well and good. Fitting in is fine. But, on balance, standing out (for the *right* reasons) is a better place to position your one, precious life. And to stand out, you have to dare to be different. And when you're different, there's a chance of NOT fitting in.

Which leads me on to my second MASSIVE TRUTH. It's something you might need to read two or three times before it starts to make sense:

If you're risking nothing at all, you're risking everything.

I don't want you to be haunted by not having truly given life a damn good run for its money. It'd be such a shame to have left adventures unadventured, hikes unhiked, dances undanced, laughter not laughed and rollercoasters not rollercoasted.

The BIG FAT LIE is that you need to work harder at keeping up. It's one of those unwritten rules that seems to have wheedled its way into too many of us. We're lulled into comparing ourselves with our tribe. . . and working ourselves to the bone in an effort to stay relevant.

Do you understand? What you are made of? The very stars combust in the night sky with the same atoms that make up your mind. Can you feel that?
Bianca Sparacino

It's time to rethink your thinking.

I've decided to take lessons from Amelie, and that means wearing my skin with gratitude rather than loathing.

My challenge is for you to do the same. Be *unashamedly* YOU.

In order to do that, you're going to have to learn to clear that muddle from between your ears, quieten the shouty inner voice and dare to leave some things unticked on your to-do list.

Darling girl: it's time to stop *trying* to be perfect and start *actually being* awesome.

Are you living the life you choose or managing the one you've got?

-Jessica Pryce-Jones

Chapter 4

MIRROR, MIRROR ON THE WALL. . .

EPIC life:

great day	great day	great day	great day
great day	great day	great day	great day
great day	great day	great day	great day
great day	great day	great day	great day

That mirror of yours. It has a nasty habit of revealing who's in charge of your life.

A dozen years ago, I decided to call mine my *accountability mirror* because I twigged that the person looking back at me was the one who was in charge of me having a great day.

Or not.

I realised that we all have special needs and the best helping hands were at the end of my own arms. My one precious life comprised about 28,000 days and if I could have more great days then I might accidentally end up having an epic life.

So I looked in the mirror and made myself some promises. No more dithering. No more *meh*. No more average. No more whinging. No more coasting. Most of all, *no more excuses*.

I set some goals, some tiny, some much bigger, and asked my accountability mirror to hold me to them.

Make my bed.
Clean up after myself.
Show up at work with a smile, and heaps of energy.
Eat good food.
No more scamming my way through the day, pretending to be working hard.
No more lying to myself.
That body of mine, get it fit.
Be a pleasure to have around the house.
Do stuff that makes my nearest and dearest go 'wow!'.

Be a super-nice human being.
Turn up on time.

Basically, I reinvented myself. I didn't become someone else, I became more of who I already was. My potential began to shape itself into something really quite exciting.

I was living with purpose. I was living *on* purpose. For the first time in my life, I was *truly living*.

And what you'll realise at the outset of personal change is that reality bites. It locks you in its jaws and hangs on tight. It's easy to revert to the old excuses and the fake you.

But in order to upgrade to You 2.0, you need to take stock of the current you. The wheel of wellbeing is designed to do exactly that.

All you need is a sharp pencil and some razor-sharp honesty. On a scale of 0 to 10, rate yourself in the following eight areas of your life by shading the segments of the wheel below. Remember, you are drawing a shape of your wellbeing right now:

1. Relationships at home.
2. Friendships.
3. Attitude/behaviour/effort at school.
4. Fitness.
5. Healthy eating.
6. Quality/quantity of sleep.
7. General happiness and wellbeing.
8. Self-esteem.

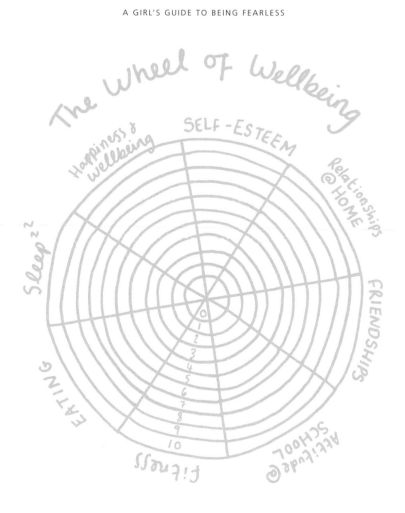

Once you've completed your wheel, you have an idea of You 1.0.

That's your starting point.

Now, using another colour, rate where you want to be on each of the eight categories.

That's You 2.0.

That's where you're heading.

Now, forgive me if this next bit of book sounds a bit tell-y off-y. It's not meant to. It's supposed to be the most loving kick up the bum you've ever been given. Because I care, it matters and you need it. *I* need it. We *all* do.

FACT:
If you keep doing what you're doing, you'll keep getting what you're getting

If aspects of your life aren't working, you need to acknowledge them. . . and take *responsibility* for them. For example, if Mrs Hutchins keeps picking on you, you need to be honest enough with yourself to accept that there's a reason she's doing it. Okay, she might constantly walk around with a face like a pickled onion, but if she's giving you a hard time, there'll be some responsibility at your end. So you've got to change something about your attitude and/or behaviour so she can pick on you for the *right* reasons, not the wrong ones.

If you're unsure, take another look in the accountability mirror. It's never wrong. It's not Mrs Hutchins looking back at you, right?

Right. . .

And if your stepdad's always on at you to do your homework, you need to understand why. Why has the poor bloke had to ask nine times? Yes, the answer's in that blinkin' mirror again!

You are stopping you. Black, white, brown, purple, male, female, fluid, straight, gay, bi, Christian, Jewish, Muslim, atheist, Jedi, short, tall, skinny, curvy, confident, nervous, shy, British, American, Outer Mongolian. . .

If you want to be the most epic YOU possible, you *have* to start by getting REAL with yourself.

The biggest myth is 'overnight success'. Lady Luck doesn't just rock up and plant a big wet kiss on your lips. If you want Lady Luck to show up in your life, you have to get busy inviting her. There's prep to be done. Lady Luck needs tempting into your life.

'Cos when she does turn up (which she absolutely will), you've got to be ready.

Job interview, uni application, exam paper, new relationship, responsibility, hard work, team captain, daring to put my hand up in science, apologising, changing my attitude, getting in shape, auditioning, living up to my full potential. . .

Mirror, mirror on the wall. . . *who's the readiest of them all?*

Children are happy because they don't have a file in their minds called 'All the things that could go wrong'.

-Marianne Williamson

Chapter 5

THE FACTS OF LIFE

The parcel of everyday life:

Stress

anxiety

A GIRL'S GUIDE TO BEING FEARLESS

It's a fact that you can't spell 'challenge' without 'change'.

It's another fact that in every town, in every land, millions roam the streets in a near zombie-like state, a thousand miles away from feeling as great as they could.

Everyone starts out the same way. You pop out of your mum's tummy and, hey presto, every single one of the 7.5 billion people on the planet started with one thing: *potential*.

Knee-shaking, awe-inspiring, mouthwatering *potential*.

In physics, there's something called 'potential energy' – energy that is already there but, as yet, is unused. And to borrow this concept, human beings, aged one day, are all bubbling with *potential* awesomeness.

What *might* be.

And I circle back to the brutal truth of a few sentences ago: there are millions upon millions of people who haven't lived up to their potential. I know, because I used to be one of them. I was *potential* potential for 30 years. I had so much capability that had been left untapped.

Just to be clear, I had plenty of excuses as to why life hadn't quite turned out as I'd hoped. I wasn't clever enough. Or confident enough. I didn't have quite enough talent. There was always someone better than me. I didn't know how or where to start. Oh, and I most definitely didn't have *time* to start. Come to think of it, I didn't have enough money either.

And, even worse, it never crossed my mind that they were excuses, or that I had so much potential to do things, be amazing, create stuff and make a dent in the universe.

But the biggest excuse (realised only through the power of hindsight) is that even if I knew how to maximise my potential, and if I had the confidence, money and intelligence – I couldn't actually be bothered to do whatever 'it' was.

Because, bottom line, whatever 'it' was that I needed to do would involve the dreaded 'ef' word.

Effort!

Even worse, *sustained* effort, aka 'hard work'.

Luckily for me, I woke up. I got bothered. But most don't.

Look around. You'll see them everywhere. They're living an okay life. In school report terms, there are a lot of people having a C+ life.

I'd guesstimate that the majority of adults are living at about 40% capacity. They're perfectly fine. And that's fine, if 40% capacity is what you're aiming for. If 'distinctly average' is your life's goal, that's absolutely grand. Feel free to stop reading and chuck this book to someone you think wants to raise their personal bar to 'world class' or 'amazing'.

FACT:
The harder you work,
the luckier you will
become

The vast majority of the population are living on autopilot. But there are a few who are extra-ordinary. There will be a handful of people in your life who are stand-out amazing. The few, not the many. This book is about them. More specifically, who are they, what are they doing to make themselves feel so amazing and, most important of all, what can you learn from them and apply to your own life, so you can be amazing as well?

The bare fact of life is that it takes a bit of effort. It's breathtakingly daring. You'll need some heart and courage. You'll meet challenges that seem insurmountable. You'll experience setbacks. This is why I called the book 'A Girl's Guide to Being *Fearless*', because that's what world class takes.

Fearlessness. Which, as we now know, has zero to do with having no fear at all. Rather, it's about having:

Courage.
Grit.
Bouncebackability.
Determination.
Hard work.
Botheredness.

Call it what you want.

There's effort involved.

The good news is that it's totally worth it!

In the last decade, rates of anxiety-related disorders in teenagers have risen steadily, particularly in girls. There are various theories as to why, from digital hyperconnectivity to heightened external pressures, to simply a greater awareness – and therefore diagnosis – of mental health concerns.

FACT:
100% of successful people have failed as many times as they have succeeded

Whatever the causes, I think it's important to acknowledge two basic facts, both of which are good news.

First, some degree of stress and anxiety is not only normal but essential for human growth. I'm going to rephrase that so it hits home: a bit of stress and anxiety is good for you. It's part and parcel of everyday life.

The issues kick in if those levels rise from 'a bit' to 'a lot'. *Prolonged* exposure to stressful situations is emotionally exhausting. My second bit of good news is that even when your stress levels become so high that it causes you to suffer, there are tested strategies for reining anxiety back in.

Somehow (and I'm not going to dwell on the how) a misunderstanding has grown up about stress and anxiety, where our culture now sees both as causes for concern. Basically – and it's happened very quickly – anxiety has become a 'thing'. Once the world suggests it's 'real' and it gets an airing on the TV, it becomes normalised. The upshot of that is that we have adults and young people who are panicking about the *possibility* of having a panic attack and anxious about the *prospect* of being anxious.

To be clear, worry is a normal and healthy function, and much of the anxiety that teenagers express is a sign that they are aware of their surroundings, mindful of their growing responsibilities and frightened of things that are, in fact, scary.

Your brain is designed to keep you safe, so most of the time 'worry' is just operating as a friend and ally to you, warning that there might be trouble ahead.

Your brain is built to make decisions that keep you alive and, as a result, *certainty* is its favourite thing. That's why humans create routines. They give you a sense of being in control.

It just so happens that teenagers' lives are filled with change and uncertainty. Your body and brain are transforming, you take the step up to big school, your academic workload increases and your social relationships can get a bit messy. The anxiety that comes with stretching to face these and other challenges is part of how humans develop character.

So, change and stress go hand in hand – even if a change ends up being positive, the act of going through it will still stress you out.

It's also a fact that sometimes anxiety and stress reach levels that disrupt a girl's ability to navigate life effectively. I'd be amazed if you managed to navigate your teenage years without episodes of tears, fallouts and emotional outbursts. Having a meltdown is actually par for the course. If you want one, have one! It's part of growing up.

What I'm trying to do in the pages of this book is reduce their intensity and frequency. But there's not much I (or you) can do to eliminate them entirely. Please be assured that if you are occasionally sobbing because someone's upset you or you're overwhelmed by the sheer magnitude of growing up, it's not a sign that you're mentally unhealthy. In fact, I'd dare to argue the exact opposite. An occasional meltdown is a sign that you're learning to get your life together.

Your brain is a bit like a plate of jelly. It's not fully set until you reach your mid-twenties and even then it remains a bit wobbly. Your teenage brain is going through a massive injection of hormones. Your brain, right now, is a work in progress – unfinished business. It's gawky and vulnerable to emotion.

During your teenage years, your brain is upgrading. More good news: it upgrades to reach maturity faster than a male brain so, neurologically, we're way ahead of the boys!

Females also have a wider emotional bandwidth, meaning that we tend to feel higher highs and lower lows than males. That's why a calm teenage girl can outreason an adult, but when you're upset, you become emotionally hijacked and the whole brain crashes into unreasonable nonsense (that might nevertheless seem reasonable to you at that time).

It can get a bit stormy inside your head and we all know you can't stop a storm. . . but if you give it some time, it'll pass. And once the emotional storm has thundered, lightninged and hailed, you'll find, more often than not, your blue-sky life will shine through. Often, your problem has completely blown away and you can see the same situation through clear, tear-washed eyes.

If you experience one of those meltdowns and you end up in a confrontation, my best advice is to apologise. Yes, even if you still think you were right!

Here's a script you'll find useful. Learn it and use it often. *'Mum, dad, stepdad, little sis, big bruv, Miss, Sir. . . you know all that stuff I said? I was being a chump. I'm sorry.'*

Of course, while it's normal and necessary to feel sad from time to time, we all know that genuine happiness is a far nicer feeling. The bottom line is dead simple: it's healthier for us to spend more time in a positive state of mind than in a negative one. Not only does it feel better, but when you're truly content and at peace with yourself, spectacular things start to happen with your life.

It makes sense to build in some recovery time. In strength training, you can't just lift weights day after day after day. To get the full benefits of the workout, your muscles need a chance to recover and repair. The same holds true for your brain.

If you accept that some level of anxiety is inevitable, you can spend less time worrying about being worried and more time focusing on how you can get back to feeling amazing.

The good news is that your mind recovers a lot faster than your muscles do. Your job is to figure out how your brain likes to recover. It's different for different people, so it's worth experimenting to find out what really works for you.

For some girls, playing sport gives them the reboot they need to focus on bouncing back. Others might benefit from watching half an hour of their fave sitcom, playing with their dog, going for a walk or listening to their favourite playlist.

In plain, simple English: you can't always control the stressors in your life, but you can have a say over how you choose to restore yourself.

It's worth noting that girls often feel stressed because they overestimate the difficulty of a situation and underestimate their ability to deal with it. If you stick with *Girl's Guide*, you'll learn some strategies, but right here, right now, all I'll say is this: when faced with a challenge, aim for courage, not avoidance. When you avoid a situation, you miss the opportunity to prove yourself – and your belief that you can't overcome it – wrong! You deny yourself the chance to realise your own strength.

I think 'courage' is the ultimate superpower. In fact, it's so important that there's an entire chapter devoted to it later on. 'Brave' is something you should aspire to be, because built into the word is the understanding that the person is scared and yet they're having a go anyway. Remember, scared is here to stay. Anxiety is part of life. It's not your job to extinguish these feelings, it's your job to develop the resources you need to march forward *in spite of* the fear.

It's perfectly possible to worry yourself sick. I think it must, then, be possible to do the exact opposite: *unworry yourself well*.

Plot spoiler alert: in the next few chapters I'm going to tell you the absolute truth about happiness, starting with it not being a 'thing' you can acquire. Neither is it about having 'stuff'.

Happiness is a feeling you can open up to. Yes, you can *learn* to let more happiness into your life.

Happiness isn't an experience, it's an *in*-sperience.

Yes, wonderful one, happiness is entirely an inside job.

Perhaps we should love ourselves so fiercely that when others see us, they know exactly how it should be done.

-Rudy Francisco

Chapter 6

BE YOUR OWN BFF

If I were to ask you 'Who was your first love?', I'd secretly hope you'd say your own name.

Self-love is powerful. Not big-headed 'self-love', as in 'I'm so marvellous, much better than anyone else', but 'self-love' as in 'I look after number one'. Self-love is the least selfish thing you can ever do or have, and if you *do* do or have it, everything else in life becomes a whole lot easier.

You literally become the living result of everything you think. So your thoughts or, more precisely, what you feed your mind. . . that's where it all starts from. If we fill our heads with doom and gloom (the news, gossipy media, negative friends, self-criticism), and if we compare what we feel we don't have to what we believe other people do, it will make us feel bad.

And the truth is that it's easier for us to think negatively.

Because from birth we've been programmed to be cautious and expect bad things to happen. This comes from the big people around us: parents, other family members, family friends, teachers (apologies if you're reading this and happen to be on that list. I'm a parent, and I'm counting myself firmly among the perpetrators!). Basically, the big people we spend most of our time with when we're children have the strongest effect on our thinking.

Now, they usually do it with the best intention: they want to keep us safe. I do it with my children and I'll bet my life that if you go on to become a parent, you will do it, too. Among the first words parents teach their kids is 'no':

'No, don't do that darling.'

'No. Don't run, you'll fall and hurt yourself!'

'No. Stop climbing on the furniture, you'll fall off!'

'No. Don't run into the road. You'll be hit by a car!'

We have to be taught that some things are dangerous, so we don't go and do ourselves any damage. But at the same time, the more we're taught that danger lurks around every corner, the more we learn to be fearful.

If you feel you've soaked up too much negativity in your life up to now, the first thing I need to emphasise is that there's no need for blame. Nobody does it on purpose.

The most important thing to know is that YOU have the power to counteract any negativity and lead a positive, glittering life from this day forward. And you can start by reprogramming your thoughts.

There's a lot written about self-harm. But the self-harm I want to talk about here is the sort that's going on inside our heads, almost all the time. It's your inner commentary, your inner voice or 'head chat'. Most of the time it's unconscious – we don't actually choose the commentary, it just runs in our heads. It's such a part of us that we don't even notice it's there.

Unfortunately, your inner voice is often full of negative babble. It's your 'I can't do it', 'I'm not clever enough', 'What will people think of me?', 'I'll never be as good as her' voice. It can be a total beast. We would NEVER let anyone speak to us as harshly as we speak to ourselves.

We put ourselves down for not being perfect. We hate ourselves because we don't think we're pretty enough or skinny enough or anything else enough. We're hard on ourselves if we don't get great exam results, or if we're not picked for the netball team or the school production. Somehow, we manage to blame ourselves for losing a boyfriend or girlfriend. . . or for not having one at all.

This inner voice is savage and will make you feel bad. It will shatter your self-esteem, meaning you'll talk yourself out of doing things before you've even tried. . . so you'll stand on the sidelines of an average life when you could have been slap, bang in the middle of a brilliant one.

I find it helps to give that voice a name. I've called mine Janet and I get great pleasure in kicking her ass whenever she rears her ugly head: 'Damn it, Janet, zip your lips!' If you give it a name, you can start seeing it for what it is: NOT. YOU.

You weren't born with this voice inside your head. It's not a part of you. It moved in, uninvited.

So *uninvite* the noisy shyster. Show it the soddin' door.

Your mind is the one place where you need to have total rule. And if the voice living in your head is not supporting you, it's time to kick it out and replace it with one that does. I can't stress enough how important it is that you do this. Because the results you'll get in your life will have everything to do with what that voice keeps telling you.

> *True abundance isn't based on our net worth, it's based on our self-worth.*
> Gabrielle Bernstein

If you think it's high time you upgraded your inner voice, here's how to do it.

Firstly, get good at noticing it.

Listen to your inner voice over the course of this week. Notice every negative suggestion you give yourself. Notice if you tell yourself that you're not good enough, or that you can't do something, or that you hate a part of yourself, or that someone's thinking badly about you.

And every time you notice a negative thought creeping in, I want you to write it down.

You see, your negative inner voice likes to go unnoticed. That's the only way it can wreak its havoc. The only way it can work away in the background, while you carry on with your day, blissfully unaware of all the bad thoughts it's planting in your head. Bad thoughts fester in the dark. And the act of writing them down is like shining a massive spotlight on the rascals and seeing them for what they truly are: complete and utter bull.

And then you can start to do something pretty special. . .

While you can't stop your inner voice, what you can do is work with it and train it to serve you better. And the way you do that is by replacing its negative chatter with something more positive. Basically, stopping those dirtbag thoughts in their tracks and exchanging them for better ones.

These positive replacements are known as 'affirmations' – positive statements about yourself that are meant to be repeated out loud multiple times each day in order to reprogram your mind to be more. . . well, positive. A lot of adult self-help books talk about these and for years I thought they were a load of old hoo-hah. *How can saying a few happy-clappy sentences out loud like a loon possibly have any effect on what goes on inside my brain?*

But what I've finally come to understand is this: while most of the population tear themselves apart in the mirror each morning, the happy few do something different. They cheer themselves on. They have their own backs. They say nice things to themselves.

People who practise affirmations tend to lead extraordinary lives, because their lives reflect what they tell their brains. They literally live out their thoughts. The brain simply believes what you tell it the most. And what you tell it about you, it will create. It has no choice.

So now, have a go at this activity.

Create a table with two columns.

Take a moment to think of some of the negative suggestions you have habitually given yourself in the past.

In the left-hand column, make a list of the negative suggestions. These could be something like:

I am not very confident

I am too scared to speak in front of other people

I am so tired/unwell/sad

I will never find someone to fall in love with me

I will never be successful

I'm not very popular

I don't like my eyes/nose/lips/hair/arms/legs

I am so stressed

For each statement, come up with its positive opposite and write that in the right-hand column:

I am a naturally confident person

I am entirely comfortable when speaking in front of other people

I am healthy, vibrant and well

I am extremely loveable

I am looking forward to a happy, successful future

I make friends easily and people always feel good in my company

Focus on the features you love: I love my lips/curves/hands/eyes

My mind and body are relaxed and calm. I am having fun today

Now close your eyes and ask, in your head, 'Where is my inner voice?' Point to the location where you hear the words.

Next, imagine how your voice sounds if it is totally confident. Is it louder or softer than usual? Is it clearer and easier to hear? Stronger or weaker? Do you speak faster or more slowly?

However your voice sounds when you're really positive and confident, imagine putting that voice in the same location where your old inner voice was located.

Open your eyes and look down at your list of positive affirmations. Repeat each of the new, positive affirmations ten times in your new, confident inner voice (eyes open or closed, entirely your choice).

How did that feel? My guess is a little (or a lot) weird. But I hope, by now, you get what it will mean for the rest of your life if you stick with it. There's a well-known saying that goes 'What you practise, you become'. While it sounds like a cliché, I promise you, it's truer than true. You might think as I did when I was introduced to affirmations, 'How can this possibly make a difference?' But practise, practise, practise talking to yourself in this way and the positive suggestions will begin to override the negative.

Like I said, some people say their affirmations to their reflections in the mirror. But if you're not comfortable saying them out loud to your own face, that's okay. You can write them down, find a quiet corner and read through the list, mentally repeating each affirmation a handful of times. You'll have a voice-recording function on your phone, so you could record and play them back to yourself when you're getting ready in the morning, or listen to them through your earphones while walking to school.

It's a powerful principle: whatever follows '*I am. . .*', we're inviting into our lives.

'I am tired, I am frustrated, I am lonely. I am bored. . .' If that's what you're saying to yourself, then that's what you're inviting in. So turn it around and invite in something rather wonderful instead.

Of course, there is a balance to this. We can't tell ourselves, '*I can eat chocolate and lie on the sofa all day, every day and still be the picture of health.*' That's called delusion.

What we're doing here is focusing on and magnifying the positive. . . to have a positive effect on our mood. . . to positively change the way we behave.

Simple! (Note: 'simple' and 'easy' are not the same thing.)

Let's end this chapter where we started. *If I were to ask, 'Who was your first love?', I'd secretly hope you'd say your own name.* Because it's really hard to give what you haven't got. If you haven't got energy, confidence, happiness and zest, it's very hard for other people to catch those qualities from you.

And why on earth should anyone else love you if you can't be bothered to love yourself?

Being kind to others is all well and good, but learning to be your own best friend might just be the best place to start.

Legal highs:

Fitness, fresh air, clean laundry, foreign lands, today, fulfilment, kindness, accomplishment, birdsong, love, friendship, blue sky. . .

Chapter 7

HOW TO WIN
THE LOTTERY

a hummingbird

a giant tortoise

your FAVE
pet

and YOU

what do you all
have in common?

Line up a giant tortoise, a hummingbird, your favourite pet and you. Good looks aside, what else do they have in common?

The answer is that they're all born with about a billion heartbeats to spare. It's why the hummingbird, with all its frantic flapping and pulsing heartrate, gets three years while the plodding, chilled-out tortoise can expect 150 or more.

It's an interesting thought that also leads to a BIG question: *What are you going to do with your one billion heartbeats?*

In the interest of setting you up for a bumper package of happy, uplifting, fulfilling, inspiring, go-getting, energised days, it's important that you understand you're not actually made of sugar and spice and all things nice.

At a quantum level, you are made of molecules. You are pure energy with a battery life of about 4000 weeks.

Just like the tortoise, hummingbird and your favourite pet, you will receive a body. It's the physical 'you', and just like a supermarket bag, your body's for life. The other thing about your physical form is that it's a gift. You didn't choose it. It was given to you. Like it or lump it, there is no receipt so you can't take it back or swap it for a better one.

It therefore makes sense to learn to love and appreciate it. Yes, even the wobbly, knobbly, sticky-out, imperfect bits. And seeing as you're stuck with your body, you may as well take good care of it.

FACT:
Right now, there's a lot you don't know. And if you never challenge your beliefs, the list will never shrink

The absolute bedrock of human flourishing is that you must take care of your *physical* self.

The three physical keys to being fully charged are eat, move and sleep. Get those right and everything else becomes a lot more do-able.

That's *eat, move* and *sleep*. Not one or two. *All three!*

Because you can't out-exercise a bad diet. And eating salad doesn't compensate for bad sleep habits.

I'm gonna remind you of a whole load of stuff that you already know. But I reckon it's a necessary reminder because, *ahem*, knowing and doing aren't the same thing.

Humans are hunter-gatherers. The world has moved on faster than we have, so nowadays we hunt and gather in the supermarket rather than on the savannah, but our bodies are built to move. I promise you, your body *wants* to be fit. If 'exercise' came in pill form, it would provide the biggest boost to wellbeing and mental health ever invented. The benefits of enhanced energy, mojo and mental health would change entire communities.

Your body is crying out to be exercised. So give it what it wants! You don't have to go crazy with it, but treat your bod to a brisk 30-minute walk every day. Or maybe some yoga, pilates, a cheeky park run or swim session. The physical 'you' will love you for it and it has the added bonus of making the emotional 'you' much more resilient.

Commit, not just for a week, but for life. Here's a super-smart life hack: Sometimes, in order to secure long-lasting permanent change, you have to change your identity. No, not literally. You don't have to march into the passport office and apply to be Esmerelda Hartington-Smythe IV (whoever the heck *she* is), but you do have to switch your thinking and decide to be a different version of you.

It's subtle, but oh so powerful.

For example, instead of thinking of yourself as *'someone who's always on a diet'*, you switch identity to *'someone who makes good choices* about food'. It's spooky, but if you become *that* person, things begin to fall into place.

Similarly, changing your identity away from *'I'm someone who hates exercise'* to *'I'm someone who looks after my body'* will reap massive long-term results.

Note: this is about a million times more powerful than it sounds when you read it on the page. Here's the bare-knuckled truth: if you look around, you'll notice some women have yo-yo dieted for their entire adult life. They have tried everything from shakes to kale, to Slimming World, to oily fish, to low carbs, to high carbs, and back again. Everything, that is, except the only thing that actually works, which is to *become the kind of person who makes good choices about food and exercise*.

Once you *become* that person and inhabit that way of thinking, looking after yourself becomes the most natural thing in the world. Exercise will start to become a natural part of your routine. The takeaway becomes an occasional treat instead of a daily splurge. The meal deal comes without the fizzy drink and crisps and, voila, becomes the real deal!

Let me share a school example. It's easy to become the kind of person who's rubbish at maths. Once that's who you think you are, you're doomed on the maths front for the rest of your life. So change your identity. If you become the kind of person *who tries really hard at maths*, or someone *who can absolutely master maths*, in a bizarre twist of the quantum universe, you will get much better at maths. And it'll happen very quickly.

The same principle applies to almost every situation you ever find yourself in. You might have talked yourself into being the kind of person who lacks confidence or who doesn't put up her hand or who is incapable of learning a foreign language or who is a bit moody or who will never learn to ride a horse or who isn't very clever.

Your identity – *who you think you are* – is something you've made up. You've created YOU. All I'm suggesting is that you upgrade to You 2.0.

I'm the kind of person who is confident.
I'm the kind of person who puts her hand up and gives it a go.
I'm the kind of person who can learn a foreign language.
I'm the kind of person who's mostly upbeat and positive.
I'm the kind of person who can learn to ride a horse.
I'm the kind of person who's clever and smart. I'm a good learner, a
pleasure to have in class.

You know what? I really like You 2.0. I reckon you're going places!

> It is not the most masculine, macho, or the ones with the biggest muscles who win. It's those who look after each other, who remain cheerful in adversity, who are kind and persistent and positive. These are the characteristics that help you, not just to survive life, but to enjoy it. And they're nothing to do with gender. The people who are successful are the ordinary ones that just go that little bit further, who give a little more than they are asked to, who live within that extra five per cent.
>
> *Bear Grylls*

Food-wise, eat good food 80% of the time. I'm not a qualified nutritionist so, again, will just remind you of what you already know. The best way to 'diet' is not to starve yourself. It's to feed yourself fully with nutritious food – greens, fruits, vegetables, slow carbs. Anything naturally orange, dark green, red, yellow or purple is generally good. Beige is generally bad.

Getting plenty of water on board is another no-brainer. It means that everything in your body gets what it needs, so you produce the right balance of chemicals (and that includes hormones, which are demented little suckers at the best of times and need all the help they can get). Glug two litres of lovely H_2O and try to avoid anything that can make you feel jittery – generally food and drink high in sugar or caffeine. I know it's a boring ask, but if your body's being nourished in the right way, you'll naturally have more energy, so bossing the day becomes a thousand times easier.

I'm 53 and I've never used 'essential oils', which makes me wonder just how essential they really are.

Dr Andy

To complete the trilogy, you *know* the importance of getting enough Zs, right?

Bottom line, sleep is the glue that holds human beings together and sleep deprivation is one of the simplest explanations for the rise in anxiety. When we're sleep-deprived, we're less emotionally resilient.

You've no doubt felt the effects of a sleepless night for yourself. Our 'always on' culture can make it difficult to drift off. . . and to stay in the land of nod once we get there. The recommended amount of sleep is about nine-and-a-half hours for teens. If you don't manage to bag those hours, your hormones, physical performance and brain function all take a hit, leaving you tired, irritable and less able to concentrate.

There was a University of Warwick study that measured the benefit of a good night's sleep and converted that benefit to cash. The boffins reckon that if you can get a good night's sleep, regularly, it's worth £200,000 of happiness to you.

200 grand!

So treat yourself to a lottery win and grab a great night's kip. These tips will help hugely:

1. Get lots of fresh air, natural light and exercise during the day.
2. Reduce blue-light exposure in the evening by avoiding electronic devices for two hours before bed (you can also install apps that block blue light on your phone).
3. Get rid of the TV from your bedroom. It's called a BEDroom for a reason.
4. Avoid caffeine at least six hours before bed.
5. Don't eat late in the evening.
6. Make your bedroom a haven – wherever possible, keep it a quiet, clean and tranquil space. If you share a room, keeping your own bed comfy and tidy can really make a difference.
7. Have a pre-sleep routine that helps you unwind: listen to music, read a book, take a bath, meditate, breathe deeply.

I guess this was another 'telling it straight because I care' chapter.

But me caring about you isn't enough. YOU have to care about you. Your mental health is tied up with your physical health. If your body's feeling fab, your emotional wellbeing will follow the upward curve.

So EAT, MOVE and SLEEP. Do all three better than you have to.

Chapter 8

HOW TO BREAK UP WITH YOUR SMARTPHONE

" we can't sleep together anymore! "
#GULP

DEAR SMARTPHONE,

Please excuse my clumsy language. This has been such a hard letter to write.

It's safe to say we've been through thick, thin and everything in-between. You need to understand that I love you. I always have and I always will.

I mean, we've practically grown up together! I can't remember a time before you existed.

But after being together for all these years, I'm going to have to cool our relationship.

But *wowza*, what adventures we've had! Remember when we met all those years ago? There was nothing smart about you back then. You were a bit basic: rubbish camera, hardly any memory, app-less.

And now look at you, you super-sexy, wide-screened beast. And sooooo many apps.

Yet somehow, over the past two or three years, something's not felt right. You've changed. It's not just your massive screen, luxury camera and lush 5G-ness.

Our relationship's become complicated. *You've* become complicated! Plus, you never leave me alone. All those reminders, emails, notifications and WhatsApp groups. And your constant buzzing. Even in the night. These last few months you've become a bit needy.

We used to be besties, joined at the hip. Literally, with you snuggled in my bag or pocket. And now you're in my hand, almost permanently. I've no idea how many times I catch your eye, but I glance a lot. I know I do. It's a reflex action, checking if you've lit up with something.

Anything!

But the worst bit is that as you've changed, you've changed me. And not for the better, I might add. You bring out the worst in me. In fact – and please keep this to yourself – I'm not sure I like me anymore?

Cutting to the chase, there's only so long that I can stay in a harmful relationship. Yes, we've had good times, I'm not denying that your camera roll has some corkers on it. And oh my gosh, we've done some epic selfies. But my relationship with you has been so full-on that I've neglected the important people in my life. I sit in the same room as them but I'm not with them, I'm with you: scrolling, swiping, double-thumbing, liking, poking, commenting, checking, following, unfollowing. And when I'm with you, I'm absent from them.

And that's not right or fair.

It's not just at home. When I'm at the cinema, I'm with you, scrolling during the slow bits. I'm with you in class, sneakily swiping under the table. I know Miss can see but she chooses to ignore it because almost everyone else is swiping, too.

We're even together in the toilet! (I've dropped you in twice, sorry about that.)

The final straw was that I noticed you were trying to wheedle into my baby niece's life. She's five months old, for heaven's sake! And already she's wanting to hold you, touch you, scroll you, chew you. . . like I say, your neediness has become a bit of an issue.

Me and thee, sometimes we can spend a whole 10 hours together. Sometimes my entire waking hours. Half my actual life. I'm not going to get those hours back. I've frittered them away. And recently, I started to add up the hours and it made me scared.

Scared of the things I *haven't done*, the sights I didn't see, the moments that passed me by and the people I neglected to spend time with. Those social media followers are all well and good and I love belonging to the different groups. But I need to commit time to the *real* people in my life. The flesh and blood ones. Those closest to me. Those who often sit in the same room as me, thumbing their phones while I thumb you.

I'm breaking up with you so I can commit to them.

And while I'm at it, there's one more thing. You're a smart phone, right? I get that you've got Google built in and the entire contents of the world are available through you. But your smartness is making me dumb. Sometimes, on car journeys, I'm sitting in the back seat, scrolling with you, headphones in. I'm in the same car as my mum but we're in entirely different worlds.

Why?

Why do you make me do that?

I love my mum. I should be chatting to her, sharing my day, the highlights and lowlights, forming mum/daughter bonds.

All those missed opportunities. BECAUSE OF YOU.

I don't want this to be a character assassination, but you might need to take a long hard look at yourself and what you've become – an all-consuming, attention-seeking flirt. *Look at me! Let me show you this! Look at this funny cat!* Ultimately, it's your possessiveness that's driven me away. You're controlling, and I need to do something to wrestle my life back.

So I'm proposing that we cool it. As I said at the outset, it's not lack of love. I love you. I'll always love you, but I need some time and space to get my head together. I'm suggesting we cut down our time together by 75%.

I already know I'll miss you and I'm certain to be tempted, so it's got to be mutual. You've got to agree to me switching off all notifications and all alerts, deleting a mass of apps, living 75% in airplane mode, and...

...I'm not sure how to say this...

...we can't sleep together anymore.

That bit's over for good. I'm so sorry. I can actually feel tears welling. You're going to have to agree to sleep on the sofa or in the spare room. You can't be the last thing I see at night and the first thing my bleary eyes lock onto in the morning. It's not healthy.

You say you're all about freedom, but I feel trapped.

You say you're all about connection, but I feel lonely.

You call yourself smart, yet you're making me stupid.

You promised to cure my FOMO, but you've caused it. I'm missing out on REAL life.

I've got a life that needs living, fully. That means I'm truly committed to less YOU time and more ME time. Because I know that a better me is the key to better relationships with my family and friends. And better relationships = better happiness.

Thanks for the memories.

Your loving owner x

A strong woman
looks a challenge in
the eye and gives
it a wink.

-Gina Carey

Chapter 9

FINDING YOUR BRAVE

FEAR

↑ it's just a tiny word!

Heads up: this is a BIG chapter about a tiny word.

Fear.

See? Told you it was tiny. Four little letters.

We are powerful beings, us earthlings. We have extraordinary capabilities and none of us comes close to using all of them.

Mostly because of those four letters.

This chapter is about conquering your fears. But, as I've already explained, it's not about banishing them altogether. Fear is useful. It stops us doing stupid things. Without fear we would have tigers as pets and we'd juggle chainsaws for fun.

I haven't written this book because I'm some sort of confidence expert. I don't have a superpower that prevents fear from ever getting the better of me. I'm human. I get afraid too.

I've written this book because when I was in my teens and twenties, I didn't just feel fear from time to time, I was crippled by the stuff. And I watched opportunity after opportunity pass me by because of it. These days, I spend a lot of my time speaking in front of large groups of people as a trainer and public speaker. So I guess you could say I managed to turn the tide a bit. But it took far more years than I want it to take you.

This section is everything I wish I'd had when my self-esteem levels were at zilch. It's packed full of hints and tips that, if implemented over time, will help you become the most assertive version of yourself, regardless of where you feel you are on the self-esteem scale right now.

> *Life is about doing the right thing, on a difficult day, when no one is looking.*
>
> Lt Col Lucy Giles

Before we go any further, I just need to point out the difference between *self-esteem* and *confidence*. A lot of people think they're the same thing when, actually, there's an important distinction between the two.

Confidence comes from our belief in our own abilities – so whether we expect to be good at something or not. How confident we feel can vary massively, depending on the situation we're in, the way we feel about ourselves on that day and what's happening in our lives at the time. Some girls are extremely confident answering maths questions in class, but super under-confident on a sports pitch, for example. Other girls are really sociable when they're with their friends, but painfully shy at parties. I know women who are confident at running their own businesses but tell me they have zero confidence when it comes to how they dress. None of us is perfect. And none of us feels equally confident in all situations.

Self-esteem, meanwhile, is how you value and rate yourself overall. 'Esteem' comes from the word 'estimation'. So it's your self-estimation. It's not about specific situations, it's a feeling you carry with you all the time. If you have high self-esteem, you feel good about who you are. You know, deep down, that you are loved, valued and worthy. You feel that you are as deserving as everybody else. And when you feel like this, you're more willing to step outside your comfort zone and try new things. Because even if you don't succeed at the thing you're trying, you know you'll be absolutely fine because you're still loved, valued and worthy. You understand that not being good at something just means you need to practise to become better. So guess what? You're not afraid to give things a go. You allow yourself more opportunity to suck at more things, so you can then practise more things to get better at more things. And then the confidence begins to creep in as you get better at those things.

Basically, self-esteem comes first, confidence follows. So that's the bit we've got to work on. Once your self-esteem is high, your confidence will grow in different areas of your life as you begin to try, practise and get better at new things. You'll genuinely start to become ten feet tall and bulletproof. Wowzers.

For the record, self-doubt will always be there. Even the most amazing people on the planet are wracked with self-doubt. Presidents are literally pooping themselves over how to run their country. Head teachers are making it up as they go along. I'll let you into a secret about famous folk, too: they're terrified of being found out.

So if self-doubt has snuck its way into your life, shove it in the back seat. Not in the passenger seat, because you'd be letting it navigate, and, for goodness' sake, don't let it climb into the driver's seat. Self-doubt is a *very* bad driver.

> An arrow can only be shot by pulling it backward. When life is dragging you back with difficulties, it means it's going to launch you into something great. So just focus, and keep aiming.
>
> *Paulo Coelho*

Before I introduce my top 10 tips to help you feel the fear and crack on anyway, it might be helpful for you to understand the basics of what's going on inside your brain and body when fear shows up.

Have you ever gone to speak in front of a large audience and felt your body give up on you right when you need it most? Jelly legs, shaky hands, mouth as dry as a pharaoh's flip-flop?

That physical reaction is down to a primitive part of your brain that hijacks your thoughts. Professor Steve Peters calls it your 'chimp brain'. It's the commentary you give yourself that's negative and nagging. If you ever think, 'Oh god, I'm such a loser' or 'What will everyone think if I put my hand up and get it wrong?' or 'I've got no chance because why would he ever go out with someone like me?' – that's the rascal!

The chimp brain's main function is to warn you about danger and keep you safe. But your inner chimp can be irrational and wild and loves nothing more than to go on a rampage. It's tough to control and does stuff you don't want it to do. When you tell lies or lash out at family and friends. . . that's your 'chimp' brain taking over.

It's the fearful, insecure, shouty part of your thinking. Oh, and in case you're wondering, everyone has it. Yes, even the girls who seem completely chilled – they're actually not. They have a shouty monkey brain, too!

You also have a human brain. It's the rational, sensible bit which sits side by side with your inner chimp. They argue a lot. Your chimp is telling you not to do stuff cos you're an idiot, the human brain is working quietly in the background, making the case for why you should give things a go.

When you're in a nerve-wracking situation, the human brain and the chimp brain are on completely different pages. Say, for example, you're about to speak in public. Your human brain stays cool. It totally gets that you're just speaking. It *knows* there's no real threat to your safety and so no real reason to be scared.

But the chimp brain is super emotional and gets spooked easily. In other words, it loves a drama. It sees that same speech as a threat to your reputation and has the mother of all meltdowns.

Here's the simplified, whistle-stop science behind what happens inside your body.

You're about to step up to speak in front of the room. The human brain ('you') quietly and calmly whispers, *'You're just speaking. That's it. You do it hundreds of times a day. There just happen to be a few more people in the room. No biggie. You've got this.'*

But then. . . the chimp crashes in: *'Oh my gaaad, this is scary. Look at all the faces staring at you. Waiting for you to mess up. Which, of course, you will. And when you do, they'll see what a great thundering walloper you are. And we'll be kicked out of the tribe for all eternity. May Day! Maaaaaay Daaaaay!'*

And she's off.

She sounds the DANGER alarm inside your brain, which triggers a squirt of stress hormone, which prompts your adrenal glands to shoot adrenalin into your blood, giving your body the message that it needs to prepare for action. Your blood rushes AWAY from parts of the body that aren't needed in fight or flight – like your digestive system, which shuts down, giving you a dry mouth and 'butterflies' in your stomach.

It then rushes TO your muscles so they come alive – your neck and back tense and your legs and hands shake.

Your blood pressure spikes, making your face flush, your neck redden and your body sweat.

It's an entirely natural reaction. It happens to all of us. If you feel like your body constantly lets you down in nerve-wracking situations, go easy on it. It's just responding as it thinks it should. Bless it.

That doesn't mean you have to put up with it, though. In today's world, with its distinctive lack of man-eating scary-toothed bear dogs, you don't need your fight or flight mode all that much. Apart from when you're in actual danger, like when you've got to jump out of the way of a car, or you hear your mum charging down the stairs having just seen the state of your room. For the rest of the time, all it does is hold you back.

But to find your brave, you are going to need to quieten the inner chimp. Gag it. Cosh it. Learn to ignore it. Cage it. Stick five bananas in its shouty mouth.

Because every time it barks orders in your ear and you obey it, the damn primate gets stronger, louder and meaner. BUT when you do the opposite of what it tells you to do, the one who grows in power, marvellous girl, is *you*.

FACT:
Some days I amaze myself. Other days I put my keys in the fridge

Every time your inner chimp tells you that you can't do something and you acknowledge the fear but act anyway, it steps back. The monkey brain gets quieter. Sometimes it sits up in amazement. *Wow, I didn't think you could but, blow me, you absolutely can!*

It's you 1, chimp 0.

The 'you' part of your brain starts to find its voice. *See. You did it and you're still alive! Which means you can do it again. And next time, you'll do it even better. You're unstoppable. Go you!*

So here are 10 sure-fire strategies to help find your Brave.

1. Stretch, but don't panic

FACT:
Growth begins at the end of your comfort zone. Stepping outside of your comfort zone will put things into perspective from an angle you can't grasp now

Looking back, with hindsight that's available to me now but had never crossed my mind when I was a teenager, I realise that people who live in comfort zones are actually very uncomfortable. In fact, you can get bed sores from lounging around in that comfort zone of yours.

Every activity we find easy or relaxing falls inside our comfort zone. Outside of that is our 'stretch zone' and, contrary to popular belief, not all stretch marks are bad! These are activities that make us slightly to moderately nervous but that we can do without going to pieces. Beyond that is our 'panic zone'. That's proper wobbler territory. Inside the realm of panic would be things that we daren't even try because the very thought of them makes us want to find the nearest cave and hide in it.

The key to growing in confidence in any area of your life is to move out of your comfort zone and into your stretch zone, but to stop before you reach your panic zone. Attempting something too scary too soon could make you crack under the pressure and give you a horrible aversion to trying again.

Ever.

But a smidge of uneasiness is a good thing. Moving into your stretch zone and doing something that unnerves you at least once a day is a pretty great motto to live by. Let's see if we can apply this to your life right now:

Think of one thing you want to achieve or get better at.

In the inner circle labelled 'comfort zone', write any steps you'd be comfortable taking towards that goal TODAY. For example, you might want to land some work experience in an industry that interests you. And if you had to take an action towards that goal right this instant, you'd be completely comfortable researching companies online and making a list of potential contacts.

For the stretch zone, ask yourself, 'What would challenge me?' Not so it feels impossible or your heart pounds at the thought of it, but enough to make you feel slightly uncomfortable. Following on from the last example, a stretch might be sending a message to a family friend or acquaintance who works in that industry, asking them for advice on who to contact and how best to go about it. Whatever they are for your specific goal, write some 'stretch' actions inside this zone.

For the outer panic zone, think about what would fill you with utter dread. Maybe it's the thought of actually picking up the phone to an adult and asking if there are any work experience positions available with their company, or sending off your CV, or perhaps it's the thought of arriving on your first day. Whatever the actions are for you, in they go. This circle is to be addressed at a later date.

Now, look back at the actions you've written in your stretch zone. What actions can you take today?

Take them.

The first time you move out of your comfort zone and into your stretch zone, you'll find it tough. But, hey, the clue's in the name! You're out of your comfort zone so *dis*comfort kinda comes with the territory. After a while, though, it'll stop being uncomfortable and become your new normal. What was scary a few months ago will fall well within your realm of comfort. And it's going to take something far tougher and scarier to get you nervous again. That is your comfort zone expanding. Your goal is to keep it expanding, which means continuing to take steps into your stretch zone. As long as you're regularly doing things that give you a little flurry of the jitters, your comfort zone will never go back to its original dimensions.

When you try something that stretches you for the first time, one of two things is going to happen. You're going to succeed at it or you're going to learn from it. If you learn from it, the next time you do it you'll be better and that thing will be less scary. Over time, you'll gain confidence in that particular thing, because confidence is a skill. It's something that you *learn*. It's not something you just *are*. So you can be confident in anything if you just keep practising.

If I boil it down to the bare bones, if you want to find your Brave, you're going to have to put yourself out of your comfort zone.

Often.

Precisely how often is up to you. Gather some stretch marks, gorgeous. I promise you, the further you stretch, the more epic your life will be.

2. Listen to the future you

You know what? Regret sucks!

I once read something that's stayed with me ever since: *Whenever you're presented with a choice, ask yourself which option you'd prefer to have taken in ten years' time.*

I love that. If we all lived by this rule, wouldn't we all be living stonking lives by the time we're 25? If you take the less safe option, 10 years from now you'll look back and be happy that you took the chance, asked the question or made the change.

It's easy to misunderstand our fear. Lots of people think, *'I'm scared of this. That means that I should avoid it at all costs.'* Not true. When we're scared of something, it sometimes means we care about that thing greatly but don't know how to approach or conquer it *yet*.

Sure, it's far easier *not* to raise your hand, speak up, make the phone call to the scary adult who runs the company you'd love to work at, and continue admiring the guy or girl from a distance.

The things that terrify you are often the things you're meant to go after. Because the fear is a sign that you care about it.

So listen to the future you. She's older and wiser.

I guarantee she'll be whispering through time: *'Do it, darling. Feel the fear and crack the hell on anyway. When you get to where I'm standing, you'll be so happy you did.'*

3. Count to five. Backwards!

FACT:

Putting something off makes it instantly harder and scarier

So far so good. Feel the fear and do it anyway kind of makes sense, but if you're anything like me, your next burning question is: *How?* It's all very well saying 'take the first step', but if fear's been holding you back until now, how do you *do* that?

A couple of years ago, I learned a hugely powerful mind trick that I've been using to get an instant confidence boost when I'm about to do something that scares me. Once I share it with you, you'll never forget it and once you start to use it. . . well, expect some remarkable changes.

I've borrowed it from Mel Robbins, who's now one of the most sought-after authors and speakers of our time. It's called the 5-second rule.

Mel happened to stumble upon the 5-second rule a few years ago when she was going through an especially tough time. The family business was going under, her marriage was on the rocks, she was drinking heavily and every time her alarm went off in the morning, she wanted to knock it across the room and dive back under the duvet.

At the end of another hideous day, Mel was watching TV and an advert came on that showed a rocket being launched into the sky.

And it hit her.

Not the rocket, thankfully. . . but a thought.

Mel decided that was exactly what she was going to do when her alarm went off the next morning. Her cunning plan was to launch herself out of bed so fast that she'd beat her self-doubt, fear and anxiety.

And that's exactly what she did.

Next day, when the alarm went off at the crack of arse, she felt the same dread she always felt but instead of hitting the snooze button she counted backwards – 5, 4, 3, 2, 1 – and pretty much sprang out of bed.

She had lift-off! It worked!

And Mel started applying the 5-second rule in other aspects of her life. She worked out that whenever an event requires you to take an action you know you *should* take but don't *want* to, time begins to pass while you mull it over.

The longer you leave it before taking action (the longer the time gap), the more likely it is that the gap gets filled with dread, anxiety, self-doubt and overwhelm and those feelings get the better of you.

So, the event happens [alarm goes off, you need to have a difficult conversation with someone, speak up in class, audition for the school production, ask something from someone who intimidates you, start some exercise, clean your room, start your homework, ask someone out...] and if you give yourself too much time to think, you talk yourself out of it. Remember that inner chimp from earlier? Your mind will create all sorts of plausible excuses [too tired/scared/busy/unwell/lazy] and the opportunity's gone. And we put it off. . . and we put it off. . . and we put it off. . . and we watch our lives happen *to* us rather than making stuff happen *for* us.

It turns out Mel had had enough of things *happening to her*.

It's such a laughably simple concept. Count backwards from five.

But it works. Every time. You get to take action *before* that shouty inner chimp gets a chance to talk you out of it. You rediscover the version of you that you used to be before your awesomeness got hidden under layer upon layer of self-made fear.

Any time you know you've got to do something but don't feel confident enough to do it, and you feel yourself hesitating, and you feel the anxiety, doubt and dread creeping in, and you start talking against yourself, stick a middle finger up to your inner chimp and go for it.

Stop the negative head chat in its tracks.

Start counting backwards from five: *5, 4, 3, 2, 1. . .*

Then do *one* thing, take *one* action. Sit up in bed, put your hand up when the teacher asks a question in class, pick up the phone and have a difficult but important conversation with someone, put your trainers on and go for a run. Whatever it is, just take the first step.

A little heads up: there are a couple of things to keep in mind when using the rule.

Don't count out loud when you're around other people, because they might think you're a weirdo.

And don't count up because that's how we've been taught to count. We *always* count up, so it's become a habit and uses the auto-pilot part of our brains rather than the part we use to change behaviour.

Now there's a whole science behind this that I won't go into here – just remember *5, 4, 3, 2, 1* – take *one* action – and your comfort zone won't see you for dust.

Here's your very own FIVE SECOND RULE contract:
I do Solemnly Swear, that from this day forward,
I will be a more courageous version of myself.

I WILL BE THE MOUSE THAT

ROARED

The FIVE SECOND RULE is <u>NOW</u> my **mantra**.
I will apply it in class, at home... in fact everywhere.
In sickness and in health, for richer or poorer, till the day I croak.

5. 4. 3. 2. 1: BRING IT ON

Sign your name _____

Date _____

4. Do it for Doris

> *You have power over your mind – not outside events. Realise this, and you will find strength.*
>
> *Marcus Aurelius*

Before every exam at school, my mum would say to me, *'The first thing you do when you turn that test paper over is swear at it'*, to which I'd promptly roll my eyes and ignore her (she likes the occasional ramble, my mum). Years later, I realised that what I thought was waffle was actually wisdom.[1]

What my mum was really saying was that whatever scary scenario you find yourself in – whether it be an exam, an interview, speaking or performing in public, playing an important game of sport – tell yourself something that sucks the power *out* of the situation and *into* yourself.

I learned to do this as an actor. Just before a performance, while other cast members were worrying about whatever big-shot agent or casting director was in the audience that night, I'd take myself off, sit calmly by myself and secretly trash the venue and audience in my mind. Instead of visualising a sea of people, waiting expectantly for me to dazzle them, I'd imagine there was a little old lady and a few of her mates sat in the fourth row, sipping gin, sucking on toffees and struggling with their hearing aids. Might sound odd, but it took the pressure out of the situation. Made it seem smaller and much less scary.

I gave that little old lady a name, actually. 'Doris.'

---

[1] *Sorry mum!*

While touring a play one summer, I shared my little trick with the rest of the cast and they happily got on board. Each night before stepping out on stage, we'd say to each other, *'Come on then, let's do it for Doris.'*

That simple sentence worked like magic to shove a smile on our faces and take the edge off any nerves we were feeling. In an instant, our energy would go from 'eeek, we're scared' to 'get us out there so we can bring the house down'.

5. Get a real perspective

FACT:
Most of the bad things you
worry about will never happen.
Most of the bad things that do
happen will never have crossed your
worried mind.

How big is the situation you're facing, really? And I mean *really* really?

In the grand scheme of things, will it even matter a year from now, or as Paul McGee likes to ask, where is this issue on a scale of 1 to 10? *Where 10 is death*.

Quite often, your brain has been hijacked and you're reacting to the situation as though it's a 9, when in the cold light of day it's actually a 1 or 2. Example: getting some homework is a 2 but you're huffing and puffing like it's a 9. In the same way, your mum asking you to tidy your room is a 1, so you really don't need to give her the full histrionics as though it was a near-death situation.

Emotions also flare up in nerve-wracking situations. Whenever I was nervous before an audition, I'd have to remind myself to get a grip, that it wasn't life or death. All I was doing was going into one little room in one little building, doing what I love in front of a couple of other people. And in a few short moments, it would be over. So I might as well grab those moments by the kahoonas while I had the chance!

There's a big thought lurking in all of this. A VERY BIG thought about a very tiny creature.

A firefly lives for just one day and one night. It glows beautifully, then goes out.

Thankfully, you get longer than that, but there's not enough time to waste being average. Life is a short and precious gift. . . so, sod it, you might as well REALLY glow.

6. Visualise a winning outcome

FACT:
Whenever somebody discredits you, and tells you that you can't do something, keep in mind that they are speaking from within the boundaries of their own limitations

Professional athletes, speakers, performers. . . they all visualise themselves smashing an event before it takes place. So why not borrow their trick and play a movie in your mind of you succeeding at whatever it is you're about to do: crossing the finish line, scoring the goal, receiving a standing ovation from the audience, getting the A grade, making your maths teacher smile with your brilliance.

If you find it hard to imagine an event that hasn't happened yet, think of a time you felt incredible doing something you've already done. Close your eyes and run through the event, moment by moment, and allow yourself to feel those emotions all over again.

Alternatively, use this technique to imagine a more assertive version of you.

Stand comfortably and close your eyes.

Take time to vividly imagine how you would be if you were more at ease with yourself than you are now. How would your posture be? Shift your body so you're standing like that now. Stand the way you would be standing if you were feeling completely attuned, calm and confident.

Now, imagine an even more confident you, standing in front of you – a little bit taller, a look of slightly more self-belief behind their eyes, emanating a little bit of extra charisma.

Imagine stepping into that more confident you. Stand as they were standing. See through their eyes, hear through their ears and feel the feelings of your more relaxed, confident self.

And notice, again, that in front of you is an *even more confident you* – with an even bigger presence, even taller, self-belief and charisma pouring out of every pore of them.

Step into that more confident self. Feel the assertiveness and charisma filling your body. . . now open your eyes and go take on the world.

7. And breeeeaaaathe

It might sound nuts, but we don't breathe as well as our bodies want us to. Our pace of life means that we snatch short, shallow breaths rather than filling our lungs with the amount of oxygen needed to make us feel good.

'Box breathing' (so-called because it involves four simple steps: inhale, hold, exhale and hold) involves sitting and breathing deeply and slowly for just a few minutes. It's often done as part of meditation and is proven to have a gorgeous calming effect.

Here are the basics.

Once you're sitting or lying comfortably (otherwise known as 'getting anchored'), place your hands either side of your belly button (it might help if you close your eyes but, as always, entirely your choice), then. . .

Take a breath in through your nose to the count of four. As you do, imagine sending the breath right down to your belly, where you've placed your hands.

Hold the breath to the count of four.

Exhale the breath gently to the count of four.

Hold the breath to the count of four.

Repeat for at least five minutes, longer if you want to. The important thing is that you feel calm and centred by the end. If any thoughts pop into your head, try not to follow them. Simply notice they're there and let them pass.

8. Move

When you're in fight or flight mode, adrenalin builds up in your body. If you stand stock-still, the pressure will just intensify. . . so move! If you have some space, take a walk. Better still, put on some music that makes you feel epic and shake yer maracas.

If you're in a situation where you have to sit still (if you're in an exam or waiting in the audience before a speech or performance), you can gently 'pad' your feet up and down to release the energy.

9. If you're going to be in the room, BE in the room

> Wherever you stand, be the soul of that place.
>
> *Rumi*

Posture matters, so take up your space. All of it!

Both you and those around you will think you're in control if you own your space. . . and look relaxed doing it. Here's how:

Find a private spot in the room, stand with your feet shoulder width apart and slightly soften your knees.

Keeping your feet flat on the floor, imagine there's a chord running up your spine and out through the top of your head. Then imagine someone gently pulling on that chord, lifting your head up high.

Now take in the top corners of the room with your peripheral vision. Stand tall and 'drink in' the view in front of you.

I find it helps if you imagine someone turning on a little light behind your eyes. And, of course, it *always* works best if you smile.

Holding an open, powerful stance like this can instantly make you feel more confident. It changes your body's chemistry by upping your levels of testosterone (confidence hormone) and lowering cortisol (stress hormone). You'll send a whole new message to the world and, more importantly, to yourself about how naturally confident you are. Enough practice of standing and walking in this way will eventually re-set your muscle memory and become your predominant habit.

You'll own every room you walk into.

10. Stop trying

We've snuck this final fear-conquering top tip in at number 10, to hide it from your parents and teachers. They'll absolutely hate it because it goes against everything you've ever been taught.

Please note, I'm choosing my words very carefully here. For the record, I'm all for effort. The 'ef' word is not just *an* ingredient in success – it's *the* ingredient.

So please aim for an A for effort. But a Z in *trying*.

I hate the word 'try'. It ruins everything!

For a number of years, I used to set New Year's resolutions along the lines of 'this year I'm going to *try* to eat more healthily', or 'I'm going to *try* to do more exercise', or 'I'm going to *try* to be more confident'. . . and every year, by January 3rd, I'd failed.

It just so happens that the same promises minus the word 'try' are a million times more powerful. I'm *going to* eat more healthily, *do more* exercise and *be more* confident. . . my inner chimp is like *wowza, you really mean it!*

Quit *trying* and start *doing* is half the story. The other half is the bit your parents will loathe. It's something you'll never read in any other personal development book, ever.

If I surveyed 1000 people and asked them to complete the saying *'if at first you don't succeed. . .'* they'd all trot out exactly the same worn-out mantra about *try try, again.*

[Yawn]

Full effort, yes. But we shouldn't get stupid about a continuous lack of success. If you're going for it, and going for it, and going for it, and going for it, and getting absolutely nowhere, sometimes the bravest thing to do is give up. Yes, you heard right. Sometimes it takes more courage to give up than to carry on.

Once again, please don't take my advice out of context. It's not an excuse for an easy way out, but there'll be some people and activities in life that aren't worth persisting with. Let them go and instead focus your efforts in the direction of maximum payback.

Here they are in all their Tweetable glory, the top 10 tips for #FindingYourBrave:

1. Stretch, but don't panic.
2. Listen to the future you.
3. Count to five. *Backwards!*
4. Do it for Doris.
5. Get a real perspective.
6. Visualise a winning outcome.
7. And *breeeeaaaathe.*
8. Move.
9. If you're going to be in the room, BE in the room.
10. Stop trying.

You is kind. You
is smart. You is
important.

Kathryn Stockett, The Help

Chapter 10

YOU. ARE. MORE THAN. ENOUGH

(and ALL the better for it!)

The older generation have invented the term 'snowflake generation', which is a condescending way of suggesting that your generation is a bit melty. Emotionally brittle. The argument is that you're okay when things are going well but when the going gets tough, young people fall apart.

I would like to unreservedly apologise on behalf of any adult who ever chucks 'snowflake' in your direction, as well as make two points that absolutely need making.

First up, those who criticise the young generation forget who raised it. If, indeed, there actually was a generation of emotionally brittle human beings, it'd be because we created them, so we should be taking a long hard look at ourselves, rather than criticising you.

Second, the world has moved on so far and fast in the last 20 years that growing up has morphed from an idyllic, no-pressure, walk in the park to a full-on, hot-house, pressure-cooker of a sprint. You are clobbered every day with images and messages that suggest 'you are not enough'. It happens so often that you listen. And you doubt. And you worry. And you compare. And you feel rubbish. Worse still, you start to believe the 'you are not enough' mantra.

If you're not enough, that implies there's something missing. . . so the logical thing is to look for the missing piece. It's not a million miles away from the fabled kids' book *We're Going on a Bear Hunt*, except 'you're going on a *you* hunt'. Off you trot, through the wavy grass, splashing through the cold river, getting lost in the deep, dark wood and venturing into the cave. . . in a never-ending search for that missing piece that will make you whole.

But if you understood that you're already enough, the search would be over.

In fact, scrap that. 'Enough' isn't enough. It's on a par with 'OK' and that, sister, is not what you are.

You are MORE THAN enough.

You are complete. You are whole. You are bang on.

You already have everything you need to take on the world. Sure, there might be things you want to hone or build upon or refine, but you're not missing a single ingredient, missus. Not one.

It just so happens the world is going to ridiculous lengths to make you *think you are*.

> *You can be the ripest, juiciest peach in the world and there's still going to be somebody who doesn't like peaches.*
>
> *Dita Von Teese*

If we really want to (and let's face it, for some bonkers reason, most of us do), we can be reminded of our 'flaws' 24 hours a day, 7 days a week. . . when we look at our phones and scroll through a Photoshopped, filtered, cleverly angled highlights reel of someone else's 'wonderful' life.

You are in control of what you allow inside your head and, more importantly, of what you allow to stay there. And because your life will unfold in direct accordance with the things inside your head, that's the best possible news anyone could ever give you.

The wonderful thing about being *more than enough* is that those words apply even in the moments when you think you're not enough.

It's perfectly okay to have a bad time. Sometimes, there's no alternative but to sit down and have a big old sob. Crying serves a purpose. It lets stuff out. It's the start of the repairing process. It can be a bit messy, but it's your safety valve.

You've learned that if you fall down and cut your knee, it bleeds for a bit, scabs over, starts itching and, eventually, you spend an entire evening picking at the scab and, hey presto, brand new pink skin.

The physical 'you' repairs itself, but what you might not know is that the same applies to your emotional self. All human beings come with a standard issue of 'ordinary magic'; an inbuilt ability to heal your heart and mind.

To unearth something very powerful, let's park the modern world and go back in time, to the Japanese art of Kintsugi.

Good and bad news: The bad news: nothing is permanent. The good news: nothing is permanent.

It's worth a Google. Kintsugi is the ancient art of gluing broken pots back together, but with a difference. Kintsugi roughly translates as 'golden seams' or 'golden joinery' because when the pieces are glued back together, they put gold colouring in the glue. The end result is that every single crack is deliberately highlighted.

The wonder of Kintsugi is this: the broken pot is deemed more beautiful *after* it's been put back together. The breakages have not ruined the pot. On the contrary, Kintsugi deems that the pot is enhanced when all its flaws are deliberately exposed.

And I can't help thinking there's something in there that's also true about people.

I have an inkling that we're all human Kintsugi. We're all broken. I know I am. But the scars, the damage, the breakages, the flaws. . . these are all part of our beauty.

Your breakages have made you who you are. You are *you* because of them.

Human Kintsugi activity

1. Think about milestones and events that have been important in your life.
2. What achievements are you pleased about?
3. What 'less than happy' experiences have influenced you? What did you learn?
4. Write a list of things you feel good about in your life.
5. What, for you, is 'success'?
6. Interviews with the elderly do not report that people have regret for the things they have done, but rather, people talk about the things they regret *not* having done. What are your thoughts on that?
7. What are the most important things life has taught you so far?

I think the human/Kintsugi analogy is powerful stuff. In fact, open the bag and release the cat – nope, *several* cats – because here's another truth you won't hear anywhere else: Kintsugi, resilience, positivity, wellbeing, strengths, happiness, anxiety – these are big chunks missing from the school timetable.

School's great at curriculum stuff. There's nowhere better for geography, science and maths. . . but you know those algebraic formulas that your maths teacher considers so vital? There's a 99% chance that you'll never ever use them once you've left school. You already know that, right?

Instead, it might have been more useful to have lessons in how to deal with hurt – and I mean *true* hurt: funeral hurt, grieving hurt, relationship hurt.

And although school teaches you Shakespeare, and you learn that *Romeo and Juliet*'s a half-decent story, it never teaches you how to love. How to *truly* love. How to selflessly commit to someone else. For life.

Your science teacher might ask you to dissect a frog, but the curriculum fails to delve into what's inside of you – your own heart and how breakable it is. There are no lessons in 'how to repair a broken heart' or 'resilience' or 'how to make ends meet' or 'what happens when that dream job never materialises'. You never learn how to get up each and every day, filled with dread for whatever lies ahead, and to keep going against the odds.

School never teaches you how to sit by a hospital bed for days on end. How to console. How to empathise. How to mourn.

You'll dabble in foreign languages but never with the language in your own head: how to live with your demons, disappointments and nagging self-doubt.

School doesn't teach you how to truly push back at life when it closes in on you.

Flip the coin, school also fails to deliver on 'how to deal with success' or 'how you should behave when your dream really does come true'.

And the biggest missing link is that nobody (not at school, college or in life) ever teaches you how to love yourself, how to build mental strength that doesn't wax and wane when the world throws its worst your way.

Which it really will.

Three truths become crucial.

First, just because you have messed up doesn't mean you *are* messed up. Bad stuff will surely feel bad. But it's part of the journey. You're learning what it takes to be human.

What it takes to be real.

If you're to fall in love with life, you have to embrace the whole show: the laughing, crying, terrifying, angry, happy, sad, joyous, embarrassing, boring and regrettable bits. That's just life.

Once this penny drops, you'll be unstoppable.

Second (and somewhat bizarrely), when you realise life is hard, it gets easier.

You are not bulletproof. Sticks and stones may, indeed, break your bones, and as for words? They're even more dangerous. You are flesh and bone and blood, with a heart made of glass. Like any emotional creature, it's in your nature to bend, occasionally to break, but always to heal.

Yes, I said always to heal.

When life has dealt you its worst, you will feel dreadful. That's how you're supposed to feel. Until your mind decides 'onward!' and the ordinary magic is summoned.

You might have heard ordinary magic called by its other name: time.

Healing doesn't just take time, it takes courage. It takes guts to pick yourself up from the wreckage, to dust off your limbs, bandage your hurts and move on. Kintsugi suggests that survival is more than burying the damage, it's about becoming friends with it.

Moreover, it's about being thankful for it.

You are damaged goods. And you are YOU because of it.

Amen.

The secret, darling, is to love everyone you meet. From the moment you meet them. Give everyone the benefit of the doubt. Start from a position that they are lovely and that you will love them. Most people will respond to that and be lovely back and it becomes a self-fulfilling prophecy, and you can then achieve the most wonderful things.

-Joanna Lumley

Chapter 11

THE CHAPTER ABOUT BULLYING

be more
Buddha

Every personal development book written for teenagers is guaranteed to have a chapter on bullying and yet, right at the start, I promised NOT to write the *same old, same old*.

And here we are, with sunrising predictability, at the chapter about bullying.

The way I'm going to get around it is by writing a chapter about bullying but without mentioning 'bullying'. So no b-word. It's like writing a cookery book without mentioning cooking or a maths textbook that somehow fails to mention the m-word.

It's quite a challenge, and I hope you appreciate the creativity that's about to come your way.

Onwards. . .

Before I introduce you to 6.5 strategies, I'd like to reminisce. I don't know how you're feeling about yours, but thinking back, I had some spectacular teenage years and some absolute shockers.

It was a mixed bag of delightful highs and sucky lows and other days that were. . . well, somewhere in-between. It's a funny old place, school. A giant pressure cooker of crazy emotions. You walk through the gates and suddenly you're in competition with everyone around you, your business isn't your own and there's far too much importance placed on who is and isn't popular.

A little heads up: beyond education, 'popular' has an entirely different meaning. It's not about how classically beautiful you are (whatever *that* is!) or how many spectacular clothes you've got in your wardrobe.

I promise you this next bit is stark raving true – one day you will have an interview that isn't just for any old job, it'll be for your dream job. In terms of the 'heads up' paragraph above, it *will* matter whether you've been popular and it'll help if you can scrub up and look smart. And your general schooling will be important. But at that dream job interview they won't ask you *'What's the chemical symbol for neon'* or *'Can you explain the subtext of William Golding's "Lord of the Flies" and how it might relate to modern civilization'* or *'Can you ask for 3 bags of sugar and a tin of evaporated milk, in German?'*.

Other things become more important. Like how trustworthy you are. How dedicated, innovative, self-assured, loyal and kind you prove yourself to be. Can you work as part of a team? Can you think for yourself? Can you bring passion, energy and positivity to work, even on a Monday? In fact, *especially* on a Monday?

And 'importance' outside of work boils down to whether or not you're partner material, or incredible friend material. Whether you'll add value to someone's life. Whether you make other people feel good and, as a result, how much they want you in their lives. Or not.

That's what's important *'out there'*.

But in the meantime, when you're in school, it can feel like a never-ending fight to the top. And those most afraid of not getting there will step on other people to give themselves a better chance. In other words, they become the b-word that rhymes with 'pulleys'.

Having a desire to make other people feel low. . . is pretty low in and of itself. It's a sure-fire sign that there's something very wrong with them, not you!

They make fun of kids who are easy targets, or they join in with the teasing, relieved that they're not the ones being picked on. The easiest way to avoid being the person who's being picked on is to be the picker-onner. That's why they all have insecurities. The picker-onners are so insecure that they have to point out other people's 'faults' (no matter how tiny or ridiculous or made up), so the attention is deflected away from *their* issues.

A person becomes one of those b-words that rhymes with 'fully' ONLY if they're in roaring pain. They make other people feel bad about themselves so that they can feel better about *them*selves. It's a coping mechanism. They don't want to be the only person feeling afraid, powerless, angry, lonely or worthless, so they try to make others feel the same way.

It's also quite likely that the mean ones are from families that are always angry at each other, so they've grown up thinking that behaving aggressively is normal. They're just copying what they've seen and, sadly, don't know any different.

Of course, most won't consciously realise that these are the reasons for their behaviour. But it's true. It comes from a very dark place of misery. It is NEVER anything to do with the victim.

Whenever I come across someone behaving like a twonk, it helps me to remember that it's hurt people who hurt people. When I recognise someone hating as someone hurting, I realise their issue isn't about me. It's 100% about them. Understanding that it's about a conflict that they haven't been able to resolve inside of *themselves* helps me look at nasty people in a different light. Instead of fear, I feel pity and sympathy.

Moreover, I feel pleased that I am not like that!

FACT:
An unhealed person can find
offence in pretty much anything
someone does.

A healed person understands that
the actions of others have
absolutely nothing to do with them.

Each day you get to decide which one
you will be

Genuinely happy, grounded, peaceful people have nothing but total love and respect for other humans. Because, of course, they have nothing but total love and respect for themselves.

Self-confidence and self-esteem should have SELF in capitals! They don't come from your upbringing, or your God, or being good at PE. . . self-confidence and self-esteem come from within you.

If you have high self-esteem, and you walk around knowing that you're valued and loved and worthy, then you won't feel the need to tear anyone else down to make yourself feel better.

There are no holes *inside* of you that need filling from anything *outside* of you.

Sad though it is, practically everyone will feel victimised at some point in their lives. But if you think about the things people are belittled for, isn't it always senseless, irrelevant nonsense? When did we decide that it was shameful to be a different size or shape, to speak in a different way or have a distinguishing feature? And to belittle someone who drops their tray at lunch or trips up walking into assembly? Have a giggle, for sure – it's funny. But have a laugh *with* them, not *at* them. Tripping up is not a crime.

How did those things ever become a big deal?

If you're experiencing any kind of nastiness at the moment, please remember that this is just a tiny slice of your time on earth. Before long, you'll leave it all behind. And once you get out into the wider world, you'll find that there are so many smashing people in it, who'll love you, exactly as you are.

Even more importantly, the things you're getting grief for now may soon be the things that you go on to dazzle the world with. Maybe you're incredibly smart, or funny, or kind, or you have a unique look, or you're exceptionally good at maths, or reading, or singing, or drawing, or writing stories. Maybe you stand up for people's rights. Or animals' rights. Maybe you're beautifully sensitive and thoughtful. Maybe the most incredibly creative things come out of your fantastically bonkers brain!

> *Just be you. And if people don't like it, then find new people.*
> Unknown

And maybe those qualities haven't been appreciated. *Yet!* But just you wait. The world is gonna LOVE you.

Yes, YOU.

With all your quirk and uniqueness and silliness and YOUness. With all your kindness and warmth and passion. So don't let people with their own deep-seated emotional problems rob you of any of the things that make you fantastically you.

That's not to say if you're being treated badly you should sit tight till it's over 'cos karma will do its thing. It probably will, but that doesn't mean you have to suffer till then. While you can't stop someone being a jerk if they're determined to be one, you can ALWAYS decide how you let it affect you and how you then respond.

So here are my top tips for when the slings and arrows come your way. Which, at some point, they probably will.

First, **stay classy**.

Being upset with them is a waste of your time and energy. Instead, plough that time and energy into improving yourself. The best way to get your own back is to stay on track to being a better version of you.

That means NOT stooping to their level, even when it's handed to you on a plate.

I *know* it's tempting to fire back a savage remark or two. Or ten. Believe me, I've been there, which is why I'm telling you it doesn't work. I've raged at them in the past. I've tried making them taste their own poison by shaming them back. The problem with that type of response, though, was that it made *me* a horrible person, too.

And you're classier than that.

So rather than lowering yourself to their level, the best thing you can do is blank them completely. Walk away. Head held high if possible. Try to keep your emotions in check if you can. Show them that they're having absolutely no impact on your life. If it helps, you can repeat *'what you think of me is none of my business'* in your head and crack on with what you're doing, while remaining the picture of calm. It will completely disarm them.

There's nothing classier than keeping hold of your power by showing poise when someone else is trying to make you lose your rag.

Second, **seek to understand**.

Remember that the only thing you can control is the way that YOU respond. Remind yourself of the reasons behind their behaviour. Something or someone in their lives has made them feel horribly small and insignificant. That's what's driving them to find power in superficial ways. I know this might seem unthinkable – and you might have to dig reeeeeeeeally deep – but try to find a bit of empathy and compassion for them.

Loving the unloved is ninja level.

Third up, assess. Ask yourself if you feel safe and comfortable enough to handle the situation. If so, skip along to #5. But if you feel scared or at risk in any way, do #4.

Which is, #4: **confide**. In an adult you trust. The good thing about school is that you're surrounded by professionals who are trained to deal with this stuff effectively. Teachers and support staff are there to protect you and keep you happy. So turn to them. They'll take the stress off your shoulders and help you figure out what to do. I know this step might make your toes curl. I get it – no one's rushing to get themselves labelled a 'grass'. But there's a simple way through that: approach the adult when there's no one else around. If you don't want them to intervene, say so. They will, of course, have to step in if they feel you're at risk in any way, but otherwise they can just be a sounding board, give you advice and keep a subtle but careful eye out. It's important that you have someone in your corner with the power to defend you if the going gets tough.

Fifth is to **talk one-to-one**. If the person usually gives you grief in front of their friends, you'll probably see a very different side to them when the audience isn't there. When you next see them alone, ask them if you can talk through the issues. Be friendly but assertive. You can say something along the lines of *'It feels like there's a lot of tension between us and I really don't want there to be. Can we talk about it?'*

Now, they could say *'no'* of course, but that's their lookout. It'll be because they don't quite know how to handle your maturity and decency. In that case, you might find that just by being brave enough to approach them in the first place (and show a little kindness), they back off anyway and don't target you again.

If they say *'yes'* and it's possible to have the conversation there and then, go ahead. If it's not the right time, you can arrange to meet somewhere a little later. Here are a few things to keep in mind when having the chat:

- Speak in a neutral space. Somewhere that neither one of you is more connected to. You don't want an audience, but you don't want to be isolated either. Find a spot where other people are happily going about their day: a quiet corner of the playground, lunch hall or playing field, for instance.

- To start the conversation, you could say something like *'I just wanted to ask if you were okay and find out if I've done anything to upset you'.* That sort of dialogue will sound confident but not aggressive. The other person will be expecting an attack, so this should chill their beans from the off and put you both in a better frame of mind for a productive discussion.

- Stay calm. Don't shout or retaliate if *they* shout. It's totally fine to feel emotional deep down. But just keep telling yourself to *'be more swan'*: even if you're going crazy 'under the water', keep it together 'up top'. Nothing in history has been resolved by shouting. Ever. If they raise their voice, let them. Once they've finished, talk softly and calmly. Again, this might go against every fibre of your blessed being, but trust me, it'll come as a complete shock and they'll have nowhere to go. They'll drop their weapons and gradually lower their voice to meet yours. And you'll stay in complete control.

- Stay equal. For you to get the outcome you want, the other person needs to feel as in control as you are. So keep the power balanced. If you lecture them, you'll get their back up and they'll either erupt or shut down and bolt. Tell them how they're making you feel when they say 'x' or 'y'. Ask them questions and listen. Stand your ground when necessary, but step down when you should, too. Nobody is right 100% of the time. And that's okay.

- Keep the end goal in mind. Are you talking because you want to tell the person how wrong they are or because you want the hassle to stop? You might never become best mates. It might be that you've got to agree to disagree and give each other a wide berth. That's fine. Be the bigger person and keep steering the conversation towards a peaceful resolution.

Yes, I know that the thought of talking to someone who's making your life a living hell might top the list of things you NEVER want to do. But you know what's worse? Ignoring it and letting that person make you feel awful for what could feel like a loooong time. So make the first move. If they refuse to acknowledge your efforts, don't take it personally. They probably still have demons to battle. . . and that, loveliest, is not something you can help them with.

Number 6 is **forgive**. Most people think that forgiveness is something you give to other people when, actually, it's one of the best gifts you can give yourself. Getting angry about someone else's actions is like holding a scorching piece of coal and expecting *them* to get burned. The only one who'll end up with blisters is you. The other person could be going about their day, having a jolly old time, while you're eating yourself up with rage. So who loses in that situation? If you revisit an old insult again and again, you will keep getting stung by it again and again. . . and you'll be stranding yourself in victim mode.

It's true that no one can upset you without your permission. But remember, part of being human is that we feel our entire range of emotions, so it's going to happen from time to time. It's fine if the upset wheedles its way in. As long as it doesn't stay for too long. No one can come and remove it for you. You're going to have to do that yourself. And the only way that's possible is if you forgive.

> *Always forgive your enemies; nothing annoys them so much.*
> Oscar Wilde

One side note to all of this is that while it's important for your wellbeing to forgive, it's also important, as far as possible, to stay away from people who are going to keep doing things that need forgiving.

Make it a rule to surround yourself with the complete opposite – people who make you feel good when you're with them. It's quite easy to let frenemies into your life without realising it. If you're not familiar with the term, a 'frenemy' is someone who pretends they'd take a bullet for you when, in reality, they're more likely to be standing with their finger on the trigger. Just a few minutes in their company can leave you feeling horrid about yourself. Get frenemies gone from your life and stick with people who genuinely care. Then you'll find you won't have to use your magical powers of forgiveness all that much anyway.

And finally, I'm calling it tip 6.5 because it's a thought rather than a tip: **be more Buddha**.

There are lots of Buddha stories, some better than others. Here's my fave:

For the record, Buddha was a bit of a guru but also an easy target for the bile-spitting brigade. Without fat shaming the guy, it's safe to say he was on the large side. Most statues of Buddha have him topless, so no apparent body image issues there then! Good for him.

One day, someone insulted Buddha. We're not sure what was said, but if this was a guessing game, it could have been something to do with his weight.

Buddha said to the fella, 'If you give a gift and the gift isn't accepted, who does the gift belong to?'

The insulter furrowed his brow. 'The person who owns it, I guess?'

'I'm not accepting the insult. So who now does it belong to?'

Take from that what you will. Personally, I think it's genius.

If you put it all together in a splurge of a summary, you arrive at this: anthropology would tell us that we undermine each other to give ourselves the best chance of bagging the finest genetic stock on the market. In other words, so that we attract a partner. Deep down you want someone to choose you, instead of the girl stood next to you.

So while the world's moved on, our human wiring is a bit stuck in the dark ages. Social comparison is still hardwired into our operating system. If we see a version of ourselves that is prettier, sportier, funnier, smarter. . . BETTER. . . we get on our guard. We become jealous. Resentful. Spiteful. Wary.

And you know what? It's exhausting.

If we focus on polishing our own glow rather than trying to dull the shine of the sisterhood, we all win.

So I want you to promise me something: don't put other girls down. Not a single one. Ever.

And remember that if someone else puts you down, there'll be a sad reason behind their actions. So squash the need to 'come back' at them.

Don't get caught up in the gossip of the day, either. I used to tell myself that as long as I didn't start gossip, it was okay to listen to it.

It isn't.

If you're standing around, allowing someone to feed you gossip – without calling it out – you're playing a part in it. You're letting the drama play out, letting it drag you down. . . and letting the poor person in question get a bashing.

The golden rule is this: if you haven't got anything nice to say then don't say anything at all.

> *Treat everybody as equal value, irrespective of his or her status or who they are. . . Never treat anybody as lesser and never accept anyone treating you as lesser. Respect the humanness of the other person.*
> Baroness Helena Kennedy QC

Look at the book cover. Read it aloud, slowly: 'A Girl's Guide to Being Fearless.' So be brave. Be brilliant. Be different. Be the one to fly the flag for that picked-on person. Say, *'I don't know Emily all that well, but she was really helpful to me in science last week.'* Or *'I've only ever known her to be nice to me.'* Be a cheerleader for people behind their backs. Or at the very least, change the subject. Better still, walk away and join a table where the conversation is more positive.

The most powerful and intelligent thing you can do is offer other girls your friendship. Only someone completely comfortable in their own skin can do that. That's the mark of a truly happy, peaceful soul.

Every chance you get to give a girl a boost, take it. If you think something nice, say it. Compliments are wasted inside your head.

Sprinkle kindness wherever you go. And not just in the direction of other girls. The entire world needs more humans who walk around being spectacular to each other.

Just to hammer the point home, I want to finish this chapter with a true story. It's about a boy, but I think you'll absolutely get it.

There was a teenager – let's call him Robbie – who was nice-but-not-cool. In fact, he was *super-nice*-but-not-cool. The thing about Robbie is that he wasn't worried about being cool. It wasn't that he didn't care, more that he couldn't be bothered with how others preened and painted and handcrafted their look. Robbie cared about other things. He was one of those kids who went under the radar. He had a handful of besties and everyone else in the school liked him – but didn't know much about him. There must have been something fishy about his home life because Robbie missed a lot of lessons, which frustrated the teachers.

His un-coolness centred on two things: his hair and his trousers. Robbie was self-aware. He knew about both. And yet he didn't change either (which, ironically, made him kind of cool).

His hair was hit and miss. Robbie's hair came in phases. Occasionally it was good, but mostly bad. And by 'bad' I mean thin, blonde and unstylish. In fact, on a really bad hair day he wore a hat. Yes, all day at school he sometimes wore a beanie because the beanie was actually more cool than his hair.

Worse still, his mum ironed creases into his school trousers. Robbie heard the snide comments. Nobody pushed or shoved him around, but there were sniggers as he got on the school bus. Creased trousers gave Robbie a geeky look. *'Those creases, dude. Sort 'em out!'*

You get the picture. Thoroughly nice lad but with inconsistent hair and bad trousers. And too many days off. That was Robbie.

And then, in year 10, Robbie stopped coming to school at all. His leukaemia had finally gotten the better of him.

And do you know what? When it was announced in assembly, it turned out that hardly anyone in school even knew he had leukaemia. He'd never announced it, never used it as an excuse for late homework, never complained about feeling dire, never skipped a PE lesson because of it. He'd not even used it as an excuse for his multitude of bad hair days!

Robbie had just done what Robbie did. He'd showed up, poorly as hell, and done his level best.

But Robbie's story doesn't quite end there. It just so happens that his best mates organised a Robbie Memorial Day, a charity fundraiser, all proceeds to cancer research. They raised £882.06 in year one, £1800 in year two, with the amount rising year on year.

Robbie Memorial Day has made it into the school calendar. It's non-uniform and guess what, every single kid rocks up wearing beanies and with creases ironed into their trousers.

Turns out Robbie might have been super-cool after all.

I hate all those weathermen who tell you that rain is bad weather. There's no such thing as bad weather, just the wrong clothing. So get yourself a sexy raincoat and live a little.

-Billy Connolly

Chapter 12

THE POWER OF NOW

happiness is always

Society is experiencing a massive 'wait problem'.

Yes, *WAIT*, not weight.

The mantra that's seeped into you from a very early age is that Mondays are bad and Fridays are good. Oh, and Wednesdays aren't too bad because it's all downhill from there. Once that way of thinking is firmly lodged in your head, it's difficult to get it out again. You become that person. You slouch on Mondays and skip on Fridays. You're waiting for life's happy hour.

For example, it's very common for young people to decide whether they're going to have a good day or a bad day according to what's on the school timetable. So, you slouch out of bed on Wednesday because you've got double maths (which you hate) and history (which is boring and you're not going to choose it as one of your options, so what's the point?).

> *I'm beginning to have morning sickness...*
> *I'm not having a baby, I'm just sick*
> *of morning.*
> Phyllis Diller

Think through that previous paragraph and let it sink in because it's a small example of how most people's lives play out. For the vast majority, the day decides how they feel. So, in adult land, most people hate Mondays because it's the start of the working week. They literally discount a seventh of their entire life, deciding to loathe it, because it's called Monday.

For a whole swathe of people, this hatred is extended from Monday right the way through to Thursday. They spend a massive chunk of their lives counting down to the weekend, accidentally wishing their lives away.

Which is why Friday is interesting. In adult land, the same as teenage land, Friday tends to be a work day. But it's a bit different. Friday somehow seems more tolerable because it's an introduction to Saturday and Sunday.

The weekend! *Woo hoo!* We come alive. No school. No work. Late nights. Lie-ins. Pizza night. Party. Netflix.

Then, before you know it, the alarm goes and you're rudely awakened to another Monday moaning.

If you're not careful, darling girl, that's how life pans out. You slip into a routine of bland thinking and even blander habits. Your mood is actually dictated by whatever day of the week you happen to be on. It's brief periods of 'Woo hoo' interspersed among a whole load of 'Meh'.

Happiness has been mis-sold to us as being 'out there' somewhere. Something you have to constantly chase throughout your life because it'll always be that little bit ahead of you. Something you'll eventually get when something else happens to you.

We go through life thinking that happiness is off in the distance somewhere. It's a place we might arrive at one day if we get some *thing* or some *one* first.

When you're at school, it's practically the way you're *expected* to think. Most folk go their entire lives kicking their happiness into the long grass.

I'll be happy when it's the weekend. . . *when* I get good grades. . . *when* I get an apprenticeship. . . *when* I get a university place. . . *when* I get through my first year at uni. . . *when* I graduate. . . *when* I get a job. . . *when* I get promoted. . . *when* I get a company car. . . *when* I find true love. . . *when* I can afford to buy a house. . . *when* I have kids. . . *when* I get married. . . *when* I get divorced. . . *when* I become a grandma. . .. *when* I retire. . .

Phew! *Then* I'll be happy.

The mantra of *'I'll be happy when. . .'* is called destination addiction.

Breaking news: it's a trap. That way of thinking isn't working!

So here's another of those grown-up points that most grown-ups have never stopped to consider.

What if happiness isn't some pot of emotional gold at the end of a rainbow? What if happiness is at THIS end of the rainbow? What if it's right here, right now and we can't see it because we're damn well standing on the X that marks the spot?

If we reverse the thinking to something that's much closer to the truth, we get this: what if being happy NOW is the starting point and not the ending point? So, for example, what if it's the happiest teenagers who punch above their exam weight? And what if it's the happiest students who do really well at uni and the happiest young people who secure their dream job and get promoted faster? What if being happy NOW is the key to finding your perfect partner? What if being happy NOW opens up career doors and a wealth of opportunities that enable you to live a full-colour life?

So rather than viewing happiness as a pot of gold at the end of the emotional rainbow – something to be chased and pursued – why not see happiness for what it is: available right now? You'd realise that the vast majority of people spend their entire life looking in the wrong place.

Mull it over. It's a bit of a game-changer. Happiness *right now*?

Wow!

But how?

The best happiness 'trick' is to wake up and home in on the spectacular stuff already going on around you. We have been given a powerful gift. It's called being alive. The grass may look beautiful over there, but the key to life is becoming a better gardener of your own patch. It's about being so busy making your own life brilliant that you stop noticing if someone else has seemingly got it 'better'. And you'll stop thinking about some time in the future when you really will start to live.

> *Paint your personality a million different colours. Leave them scratching their heads, unsure of how to handle the magic that you are.*
>
> *Nikita Gill*

Here's another biggie, something that's quite simple to understand but very easy to forget. I'm going to do my best to explain 3000 years of Eastern wisdom in a few short paragraphs.

Your entire life is lived in the present moment. All you ever have is 'now'. Sure, it seems like you have a past and a future but, actually, you can only ever experience your past from THIS moment. So your memories of last weekend or last summer's holiday can only be lived in this present moment. And your future. . . that never really exists. Yes, it takes a bit of getting your head around, but the weekend that you're so looking forward to isn't in the future. Because when you arrive at it, and are experiencing it, it will be your *present moment*.

So your entire lifetime is lived in a place called 'now'. *Now* is all you ever have.

It just so happens that your brain is super-brilliant at making you irritated with the present moment. It makes you impatient with THIS moment because there might be a better moment over there, so you rush headlong through life, chasing a better moment, when the truth is that you need to befriend *this* moment.

Because *this moment* is all you've got.

If that's true (which it absolutely is), the logical conclusion and the biggest concept in the entire book is this:

Falling in love with NOW is the key to falling in love with life itself.

There you have it. That's a lifetime of Eastern wisdom in two minutes flat. Life's happening now, right where you are. When you truly grasp that, you'll feel a sense of calmness. You'll have happier thoughts and feel better about yourself, which means that the world will respond to you in a better way. It's sometimes called the Law of Attraction. It means more opportunities come your way and your life will unfold more brilliantly.

Searching for happiness somewhere else is like looking for your glasses, then realising they were on your head the whole time. So take the spectacles off your forehead and put them firmly where they're designed to be and have another close-up look at NOW.

You have so much to be thankful for. Stop and think about it for a moment.

We have so many things that a large percentage of the population would give everything to have. It could so easily have been different. We could have been born into another country. The fact that we weren't is entirely down to luck. We are so LUCKY!

But human nature is to take this for granted. We get used to the good things.

One of the quickest and easiest ways to get the warm, glowing, happy vibes is to focus on what we have RIGHT NOW. If you can connect to that feeling, it'll change your life.

This is a great thing to do at the end of each day: recall the moments in the last 24 hours that brought you a bit (or a lot!) of joy. It can be absolutely anything, big or small.

In this activity, list 10 things you really appreciated today but may have taken for granted. Next to each item on the list, write the reason you were grateful for it.

If you're new to gratitude journaling, this can be a bit daunting, so I've included a few examples to get you started:

Today, I'm grateful for. . .

My bed because it gave me the loveliest night's sleep, so I was rested enough to take on the day.

The chat I had with Lilly at break because it reminded me that she's always got my back.

The help I got from Mrs Jones in science because balancing equations now finally makes sense.

My winter coat because it kept me warm on the freezing walk to school.

My dad for washing my PE kit because it was beginning to funk in a way that no body spray could hide!

My mum for helping me out with my coursework because I was proud of what I handed in.

The home I came back to at the end of the day because it's where I feel safest.

My little brother because, regardless of the type of day I've had, he always makes me beam.

Now, it's your turn. . .

1.

2.

3.

(Continued)

4.

5.

6.

7.

8.

9.

10.

It really can be anything: an experience you had that made you feel amazing, something you accomplished, a stranger who smiled and brightened your day, a hobby you got to practise, or a mistake you made because it taught you something important. You could even be thankful for someone you didn't get along with, because they made you fight the urge to flick them in the face. . . and you therefore grew in patience! If you struggle, go ahead and throw in some smaller things: your toothbrush because it will have saved your teeth from holes. . . Netflix. . . custard. . . whatever you were happy to have in your life that day.

Then, once you've written your 10 things, go through them one by one. Allow yourself a few seconds to focus on each item on the list. Long enough to feel the gratitude right down in your belly. (Little clue: if it doesn't make you smile, you haven't given it long enough.)

This activity is borrowed from actual therapy. It's tried and tested. Thinking about what you're grateful for each day and taking the time to write those things down allows you to give headspace to each one. It means the great things in your life won't just pass you by anymore. You'll notice them. And you'll realise that even if you've had a shocker of a day, you've actually got a fair amount to be happy about.

As you keep practising, you'll learn more about what brings you joy, so you can start focusing your time and energy on the things that make you the happiest/best version of yourself.

There are absolutely no rules to gratitude journaling. It's for your eyes only, so do it in a way that makes you happy. If you love to doodle, feel free. If you're a visual person and want to add photos, crack on! Why not make a gratitude journal-scrapbook hybrid?

Gratitude is the healthiest and most beneficial of all human emotions. It's like fertiliser for happiness.

Oh, and one more thing. What most people don't realise is that feeling amazing right now, in this very moment, also affects your past and future. It's like putting on a pair of rose-tinted past and present specs. When you feel great in THIS moment, your past seems kind of okay, too. All of a sudden, those bad times don't seem so bad and you dealt with those challenges pretty well and those embarrassing moments were, in hindsight, really quite funny.

Those rose-tinted spectacles also make the future seem kind of doable. When you feel amazing in THIS moment, your brain opens up to future possibilities. All of a sudden, those possibilities seem possible. Your huge goals seem achievable. And you feel confident that you can take whatever the world throws at you and groove with it.

Feeling amazing NOW gives your past a rosy glow and unlocks a future bursting with multicoloured possibilities.

In times of grief and sorrow, I will hold you and rock you and take your grief and make it my own. . . And, together, we will make it through the potholed street of life.

-*Nicholas Sparks,* The Notebook

Chapter 13

WHEN THE GOING GETS STUPIDLY TOUGH

In a book that's essentially about positive emotions, I've already made sure to acknowledge that being sad is an important part of being happy. A life of unbridled joy would be bizarre. A permanent high? You'd lose perspective.

Lows are inevitable. But there are lows and there are *looooows*.

Rock bottom is a bad place to be. So, before I give you a whole load of ideas about how to point a *normal* low to the exit, I am morally obliged to give advice about how to deal with a *looooooooow* low.

If something's troubling you and you suspect it might be more than an 'off day', here are my three top tips:

1. Talk to someone.
2. Talk to someone. . .
3. . . . and for goodness' sake, *talk to someone*.

If I was to add a fourth it would be 4. TALK TO SOMEONE. In fact, you can probably guess my entire top 10.

I can't say it enough. You NEVER have to face a *loooooow* low alone. Just speaking about your feelings out loud, to another pair of ears, has an astonishing healing power.

Negative thoughts thrive in silence. They can make you feel that you're on your own. That no one could possibly understand because you're the only one going through what you're going through and the only one feeling what you're feeling.

Darling, listen up: That. Just. Is. Not. True.

Anything you've ever felt has been felt by countless people before you (no matter how bad or weird or dark or tragic or embarrassing you think it might be). We have *ALL* been in the depths of despair and seen no way out. We've *ALL* done things we're not proud of. We *ALL* have our secrets and our troubles and our mistakes. We've *ALL* been ridiculed and shamed.

A little note on shame while we're on the subject, because I think it's the emotion we feel the hardest, carry the longest, but know least how to handle.

The definition of 'shame' is feeling bad about *who* you are. In other words, the things that make you *you*: your appearance, ability, background, social or financial status, etc.[1] Being shamed by someone is nothing short of a trauma. Without exception, the person doing the shaming is the one who's messed-up and poisonous, but it's the person being shamed who feels they're in the wrong. The last thing they want to do is tell someone because that would draw even more attention to the thing they've been ridiculed for. It would mean further discussion about it, which would only prolong the humiliation. So the victim withdraws into themselves instead and tries to recover from the pain without anyone noticing.

I could only have written the previous paragraph if I'd been shamed myself. (I have, as it goes. Many, *many* times about many, *many* things.) And I'd only write about it in a book if I thought every single reader would relate because they'd been shamed too. See? We're so similar, you and me. . . you, me and everyone who ever stepped foot on the planet.

Everywhere you turn, there are people who will understand. When you think you've hit rock bottom, speaking about your feelings out loud helps you see them for what they are – temporary glitches that pale into insignificance compared with the many brilliant and beautiful years stretched out ahead of you. And you also start to realise that others have been where you are now. And they came through it, just as you will. But you've got to make a bit of noise first. Or no one will know you're hanging on by your fingernails, so no one will throw you a rope.

And here's another thing: asking for help is not a weakness. It's an almighty strength. It shows that you know something isn't right and you want to sort it out so you can get on with your life. And your courage

---

[1] *Not to be confused with 'guilt', which is feeling bad about something you've done.*

to speak out helps countless others, because you'll be blazing a trail that makes it easier for them to follow.

You can reach out to anyone you trust: a good friend, family member, dedicated wellbeing professional at your school, teacher you get along with, your GP, the list is endless.

If you don't want to talk to someone face to face, you don't have to. There are some fantastic text and phone services on hand to help around the clock – you'll find more info at www.fearlessgirls.co.uk.

Now on to strategies for an *ordinary* low.

This chapter needs to be read in conjunction with Chapter 7: How to win the lottery. That covers the basics of eat, move and sleep. If you get those three little rascals right, everything becomes a whole lot easier.

Here are an additional top 10 tips for when the going's got tough and you need to be tough enough to get going.

They're all 'DOs', except the first, which is a 'DON'T'.

1. Don't be a carpet sweeper

So-called 'negative emotions' have their uses. If they didn't, evolution would have got rid of them yonks ago. Feelings like anger, fear and disgust trigger the fight, flight or avoidance responses that keep us safe. And though it might be hard to believe, sadness is just as important.

It helps us come to terms with bad situations, process them and move on. Like a little internal alarm, it reminds us to take a step back, absorb what's happened and lick our wounds so we can get back in the game. When you look at it like that, sadness is actually pretty crucial for our health, an important protective mechanism that allows us to heal when we've taken a hit, so we can come back stronger.

Being in a sad mood is also an important cue to other humans. It alerts them that one of their tribe has disconnected, which triggers their concern and empathy, so they reach out to help. Without even realising, sadness is our body's way of raising a flag and shouting, 'Hey, (wo) man down!'

And come to think of it, how many epic musicians or artists have said that it took a period of heartbreak for them to produce their best work? Kinda suggests that it's not all bad for our creativity either.

A little bit of gloom can boost our motivation, too. When we feel happy, we naturally want to hold on to that terrific feeling. Happiness signals to us that we're in safe territory and that we don't need to change anything. Sadness, on the other hand, can act as a warning sign that all is not well and gives us a nudge to fix what's wrong. We're forced to put effort into changing our unpleasant circumstances. So being in a funk can actually give us the kick up the bum we need to turn things around.

Despite the many upsides of feeling down, we live in a culture that values 'positive' emotions more than 'negative' ones. Which means we can feel pressured to *appear* happy all the time. We worry that if we put our misery on display, it might make other people uncomfortable. So we keep our sadness to ourselves, sometimes even *from* ourselves. We sweep the emotion under the carpet in an attempt to hide it from view.

The problem is that one day, the carpet will get lifted and all that damned sadness is still there, and it's been festering and growing teeth so it can come back and bite us on the bum.

The key message here is this: don't push away your sadness. It shows up for good reason: to tell you something. So hear it out.

Here are three more very important words: IT. WILL. PASS.

As long as you listen to your sadness and respond in the right way, another emotion will soon take its seat, most likely a friendlier one that'll take you to a much better place.

2. Make loving choices

When you notice your mood take a dive, of course the most important thing is that you do what's right for you. Self-help is called SELF-help for a reason. So before doing anything at all, it's good to ask: *is this a loving choice for myself?*

For example, is staying up late and scrolling through social media a loving choice? Or might it be that resting and going to bed earlier is a more loving choice?

It brings me full circle to Chapter 6: Be your own BFF. If you wrap yourself up in enough of your own kindness, you won't be in as much need of it from anywhere else.

3. Go with it

> *Don't wipe my tears away. I want to feel them on my face.*
>
> Henry, two years old (from @livefromsnacktime on Instagram)

Put on some music that reflects your mood, light a candle and just sit with your feelings. Try not to throw any judgement at them. They're not *good* or *bad*, they just *are*. . . so let them be. It's absolutely fine to wallow for a bit, before doing something to lift yourself back up. When you sit with your sadness, you realise that it actually has lots to tell you. It can tell you about your desires and needs, the loved ones you'll never stop missing, and it can give you information that helps you make important decisions.

4. Meditate

You'll probably be in one of two camps when it comes to meditation. Either you're already an avid fan or the next time you hear someone say 'namaste' you'll want to punch them on the nose. I was in the second camp for years before giving it a try. There are countless books, blogs, vlogs and apps about meditation, but simply put, it is time spent being still.

The *awareness of being aware* is the oldest happiness trick in a very old book, but you know what? It's never been so applicable. It is the *best* way to check out of the daily madness, to focus on here and now, without being a slave to any rings or pings or buzzes (as long as your phone isn't next to you while you're doing it, that is). It does the world of good to every single part of your mind and body. If you want to give it a go but don't know where to start, there are lots of free guided meditation apps that will coach you through it. So yes, we are generally asking you to use your phone a bit less, but a meditation app is a good use of tech. Or you could just sit/lie comfortably and. . .

5. Box breathe

Yep. This one again. It works every time you need to feel better, calmer, stronger or more focused. You know the drill. . . hands either side of your belly button, inhale for four, hold for four, exhale for four, hold for four.

Repeat.

Get that breath right down into your belly.

You're back in the game.

Both meditation and box breathing force you to do something that's wonderfully good for you: be still, disconnect from the distraction 'out there' and connect to you instead. It gives you a peace and clarity that you just can't get when you're caught up in the distractions of the day. Simply because you can't focus on your breath or any of your other senses and focus on your thoughts at the same time. Many people find that some of their best ideas come to them during these periods of stillness. It's like you're finally hushing the world up and giving yourself space to discover who you were before it got hold of you and programmed you to become something else.

A little note, though: this doesn't come naturally to any of us, so don't worry if you find it tough. If your head fills with chatter (which it will), just keep bringing yourself back to focus on your breathing. But. . . you guessed it. . . keep practising! It'll soon become addictive.

Though I reckon it's the best addiction you can possibly have.

6. Write a journal

Writing your thoughts and worries in a journal is a great way of getting them out of your head. Left alone up there, they like to fester. Even the smallest of worries can grow into massive humdingers the more you think about them. But when a worry is written in front of you on paper, it becomes a physical thing. You can see that it's far smaller than you and, suddenly, it's more manageable. You can crush it, no fear!

Sometimes we don't even *know* what's upsetting us and the simple act of writing stuff down can help shine a little light on the problems so we can come up with ways to resolve them. And you can tell a journal absolutely anything and get zero judgement back. The perfect confidante! No rules to this one at all – you can write in a book or just on paper and it doesn't have to follow any structure. It's your own, private place to scribble whatever you want. Let the words flow freely and don't worry about spelling or grammar or what other people might think. It's for your eyes only. Carve out a few minutes every day to write and think of it as relaxation time, set aside, just for you, to destress and wind down. You'd be surprised at how well you get to know yourself by diving into your deepest, most private thoughts and feelings. Write in a place that's comfy and soothing, maybe with a cup of your favourite hot drink. And be proud that you're doing something good for your mind and body.

7. Connect to nature

It just makes sense, doesn't it? Given the choice between two views; beautiful trees or a brick wall, which would you choose? Humans love being in nature. It restores us psychologically and physically. It ups our happiness levels, relieves stress, improves our memory and concentration, strengthens our immune system and keeps us fit and young. Research suggests that it has a serious healing effect, too. Studies on post-surgery patients show that those exposed to more natural light heal quicker and report less pain. It's literally a wonder drug. However you do it, whether it's a walk to and from school or a sit in the garden, get your daily fix!

8. Be a RAKtivist

You can perform Random Acts of Kindness (RAKs) in lots of different ways and get an unbeatable buzz doing it. Studies have shown that putting the wellbeing of others before our own without expecting anything in return (or what's called 'being altruistic') stimulates the reward centres of the brain. Those feel-good

Kindness is free. Sprinkle that stuff everywhere.
Unknown

chemicals flood our bodies, producing a kind of 'helper's high'. Just this evening, I watched a news story about a nine-year-old girl who makes up lunch boxes every Saturday and delivers them with her mum to homeless people in her local town centre. How awesome.

But it doesn't have to be anywhere near as newsworthy. Every little gesture counts! You might let someone in front of you in a queue, take part in a fundraiser, show a new student around your school or make a cup of tea for a family member without them having to ask. The aim is just to lift the mood of people around you. You'll be surprised how quickly you fall in love with being a RAKtivist and feel compelled to do a good deed every day. Just imagine a world where everyone made that their aim.

9. Do more of what you love

Having fun is the ultimate tonic (as long as it's YOUR idea of having fun). When you're not feeling on top form, do things that make you feel comfortable and confident. Not sure what you love these days? Try new activities. Drop in on an acting class, have a go at a new sport, join a debating team or become a member of a singing group. Anything that makes you part of a community is especially good for your mental health.

A year after moving to a new village, I was feeling a little isolated and still didn't know anyone nearby. After looking up things to do in our little village bulletin, I trotted down to the community centre to suss out the local acting group. They were an eclectic bunch, ranging from about 14 to 80, and a snap judgement nearly had me walking out the door as quickly as I had walked in – it definitely wasn't the place for me! I thank my lucky stars that something forced me to stay that night because, it turns out, that 'eclectic bunch' had some real gems in it. Instantly, I had a gang of new friends living on my doorstep, and a whole new home-life experience. I hold those gorgeous folk dear to this day. So check out what's going on around you and don't be afraid to jump in. You can jump right out again if you discover it's not your bag. Nothing ventured, nothing gained.

10. Get lost in a good book

I feel like typing this one in capitals. Magic can happen when you plunge into the pages of a brilliant book. It literally makes your brain come alive! Something uplifting or developmental can bring you into a more positive headspace in no time. Don't worry if you don't think reading's your thing; there are lots of titles also available in audio and that's a good place to start. If you're ever feeling down or a little lost, a great self-help book can really talk to your feelings and offer a bit of guidance on what to do next. Or a gorgeous piece of fiction can lift your mood in minutes, providing the best form of escapism there is.

I'm adding a wonderful bonus tip. When you're stuck, low, sad, angry or just plain ground down by life, imagine your very best friend was feeling this way. What advice would you give to *them*?

Top tip #11, **take that advice**.

My mind is like my web browser; 19 tabs are open, 3 are frozen, and I have no idea where the music is coming from.

-Unknown

Chapter 14

GET WELL SOON

Gratitude is life's
fertiliser for
happiness

When an epidemic leaks out of a community and infects the world, it becomes a pandemic. Last century, Spanish flu morphed from epi and became pan. More recently, COVID-19 did the same.

And yet, we hear very little about a pandemic that's been sweeping the globe at an alarming rate. A disease that eats away at our self-esteem, destroying us from the inside out. It causes anxiety and self-loathing in millions of people *worldwide*. And while most pandemics affect the oldies, this one targets the younger generation, with teenage girls suffering worst of all.

Largely unreported, this silent killer is COMPARE-13 (named after the age it kicks in). You might know it by its other name: Comparisonitis.

You'll know if you've got it. The symptoms include an overwhelming sense of unease, restlessness, and a bad case of wanting stuff. Lots of stuff. The *latest* stuff. Other people's stuff.

Other people's *lives!*

If you catch even the mildest form of Comparisonitis you'll feel envious about everyone and everything: lunch envy, flat tummy envy, holiday envy, boyfriend envy, girlfriend envy, hair envy, boob envy, beauty envy, sport envy, trainer envy, outfit envy, number of social media followers envy – you name it, there's an envy for it.

Comparisonitis messes with your thinking. Sufferers will gaze at filtered, airbrushed perfection and will want *that* body and *that* life – not the 'imperfect' bod and 'average' life that they actually seem to inhabit.

Yes indeed, COMPARE-13 can make you feel really low.

The worst thing about Comparisonitis is that it causes you to behave in strange ways. Like moths to a flame, you'll be drawn to celebs. Beautiful ones. Reality TV – the *least real thing ever* – becomes compulsory viewing. It actually seems real. You might feel the need to watch hours upon hours of videos of 'influencers' putting on make-up.

Sufferers' defence against the dark art of fakery is to *attack* with an even faker portrait of their own existence. COMPARE-13 sufferers will spend hours finding the perfect camera angle and pouting for the ultimate selfie. They will be experts at filtering. Comparisonitis often comes with an associated desire for a piercing, tattoo, or other form of body 'enhancement'. Sometimes this desire builds into a longing. A craving. A must-have.

Psychologists report seeing more Comparisonitis in their patients. Dr Windy Dryden (actual real name) suggests that at a *logical* level, COMPARE-13 victims know that images are filtered and that people are presenting the very best take on their lives, but on an *emotional* level, it's still pushing their buttons.

Social psychologist, Sherry Turkle (again, real name) hints at something even weirder. In fact, it's bonkers. COMPARE-13 sufferers post the best of the best, creating an illusory 'highlights reel' that they put online but, wait for it. . .

. . . they then look at the fake lives they have constructed online and STILL feel a sense of disappointment. Hang in there, because here comes Comparisonitis in all its bare-knuckled ridiculousness – they feel envious of the fake life that they've created.

Yes, you have to let that one sink in. Comparisonitis sufferers become envious of the fake version of themselves that *they* created in the first place!

I told you it messed with your mind.

So there you have it. My fake report on a fake condition, created to highlight a real issue. 'Comparisonitis' might not be an actual real word, but 'envy' is. And 'social comparison' comprises two very real words. And that's my point. Wishing you were living someone else's life is, in most instances, just a little bit sad. It means you've not truly woken up to the magnificence of the life you're *actually* living.

But in really bad cases, social comparison shows up in self-harm and a whole raft of eating disorders.

No laughs there.

Good news. There is a cure, an *oh-so-simple* remedy that will rid you of the milder form of Comparisonitis. This two-step medicine will shift the feeling in a couple of weeks.

Step one, you need to write a list of 25 things that you really appreciate but take for granted. Phrased differently, what have you got to be thankful for? Or, differently again, what 25 things/people are you lucky to have in your life but might have taken your eye off?

Anything goes. Mine would include my girls, a husband who attempts DIY and loves me even when I'm in a grump, a roof over my head, central heating, hummus, olives, the NHS, the ability to read, freedom, my ankles, Netflix, books, theatre, the ability to see, Amazon, a comfortable bra, bees, the ozone layer, goat's cheese (all cheese actually). . .

But it's your list, so get cracking below:

1.
2.
3.
4.
5.
6.
7.
8.
9.

10.

11.

12.

13.

14.

15.

16.

17.

18.

19.

20.

21.

22.

23.

24.

25.

Part one of the cure for Comparisonitis is to look at your list *every day* and marvel at what you *already have* in your life. This basically makes your envy less green. It lowers it from FLUORESCENT RAGING VIBRANT SHOUTY GREEN to something more manageable, like that nice colour that garden sheds sometimes are. I've just looked it up – fresh rosemary. *Aaahhhh*, that's better. I can cope with that.

I promise you, most people spend a massive amount of their time grumbling about what they *haven't* got, whereas your list of 25 should prod you in the other direction. I've said it before, but it's so worth saying again: gratitude is life's fertiliser for happiness. So, gorgeous girl, refocus your attention on what you *have* got and instead of lusting after someone else's life, start to realise how lucky you already are.

The second part of the cure is more painful. In fact, it stings a bit. It starts with daring to understand what your envy is telling you. Why are you lusting after a celebrity life? Why are you wanting to scratch people's eyes out?

FACT:

Everyone you meet is better than you at something. We all have different strengths. What worked for someone else might not work for you

The pain kicks in when you dare to ask, *what if it's not about them?* And the stinging starts with, *what if envy might be a sign that I need to have a good look at myself?*

Yes, that level of honesty is gonna make your eyes water!

Comparing *yourself* with *yourself* is the magic sauce. So instead of comparing yourself with someone else, you get to ask a much better question:

Am I a slightly better person than I was yesterday?

Yikes! Told you it was a biggie. If you can answer 'yes' to that on a regular basis, you'll be growing. Keep at it, daily. As your self-esteem blossoms, your Comparisonitis will melt away.

In summary, your prescription for COMPARE-13 is this:

Be grateful and be a tad better than you were yesterday. Just a smidge.

Repeat. Daily.

Doctor's orders!

Wishing you a speedy recovery. Get well soon.

Thought for the day:
Attitude is infectious. . . is yours worth catching?

Chapter 15

GOING VIRAL

Wouldn't it be a shame to have a wonderful life and not notice?

A lot of people do. Have a wonderful life, that is. And not notice. They grumble about their wonderful life instead.

Reflect on first thing this morning. Did you rise and shine. . . or rise and whine?

Exactly!

The 'rise and whine' thing. It's a very easy habit to get into, which is why nearly everyone does. But you're not 'everyone'. You're you. You're going to be extinct in the next 80 years. You're the last one of your kind left in the wild. You owe it to your species to be lively, interested and positive.

It's worth noting that what you do every day matters more than what you do every once in a while. But there's something even bigger than you. It's called 'family'. And there's something even bigger than family. It's called 'society'. And there's something even bigger than society. It's called 'humanity'.

FACT:
Your energy introduces you before you even speak

If you want to do your bit for humanity, this is how. . .

Steve Head encourages people to GOB on their friends. That is, give them a Glimpse Of Brilliance. Emotion creates motion. By that, I mean that your behaviour is driven by your feelings. So you don't really want a phone upgrade, you want the *feeling* of having a lush new unscratched screen. You don't really want Nutella on toast, you want the *feeling* of sinking your teeth into it. You don't really want that new top, you want the *feeling* of wearing it on Saturday night. Same with those trainers, that snuggly old jumper and a good grade in English.

You get the point. Everything you do, you do for a feeling, and at the most basic level, we're driven towards good feelings and away from bad ones.

The thing about emotions is that they're hugely important, but not actually real. I mean emotions aren't a 'thing' at all. They don't have a form or a shape. You can't put your feelings in a wheelbarrow and cart them around. They're triggered by events 'out there', which create thoughts in your head, which become feelings in your bod.

There are whole libraries written about this stuff, but I promise you, the previous paragraph is basically it.

Next up, our superior human brains give us massive processing power, but they are also constructed to *transfer* emotions. At its simplest level, someone smiles because they feel happy – you mimic the smile and also feel happy. (Oh, and here's a top fashion tip that the adverts never tell you: *a smile is the sexiest thing you will ever frickin' wear.*)

The contagious nature of emotion plays a big part in our survival: one hunter feels fear and the others tread more carefully as a result – it all makes perfect evolutionary sense. Emotional contagion also helps us build communities and relationships – love, empathy, happiness, these bind us together.

So second base is this: *you are contagious!*

In fact, I'll go further than that. The absolute truth is that you cannot NOT have an emotional impact on those around you.

It works via mirror neurons, which means we're compelled to copy others' emotions and behaviours. It helps us get 'in synch' with the person feeling the emotion, and once we've tuned into someone and we're on the same emotional wavelength, we've created empathy.

FACT:
Your success isn't just about you. It's about how you positively impact the lives around you

Put these paragraphs together and you get a mix of good news and bad news.

It's great that (generally speaking) the female of the species is able to 'tune in' to emotions better than the male. Ladies: it's our sixth sense. It's called 'female intuition'.

But remember, we also (generally speaking) experience higher highs and lower lows. A girl having a good day is a joy to behold. You will light up your classroom, friends and family.

And, *ahem*, a girl having a bad day. . . it hardly bears thinking about. Your toxicity becomes like second-hand cigarette smoke, negatively impacting everyone you meet.

It is truly a case of leading by example. Your attitudes and behaviours are infectious. I guess the million-dollar, double-barrelled question is: who will you 'emotionally infect' and what will you 'infect' them with?

Which brings me onto family and school. To make my point, it's helpful to think of any social situation as a soup – an *emotional* soup – in which everyone is adding some sort of 'flavour'. Take your family situation as an example. When you're all together, everyone's having a say in whether the family atmosphere is working. *Or not!*

So you've got to ask yourself what flavour *you* are adding to your family soup. Are you coming through the door with joy and enthusiasm or are you poisoning the family atmosphere with toxicity?

And second, not all family members are equal. Yes, everyone is adding something to the emotional soup, but I've just read a research report that says. . . wait for it. . . *a teenage daughter has the BIGGEST impact on the atmosphere at home!*

Oh my goshness! YOU are the main ingredient!

Your emotional contagion is MASSIVE.

I'm not going to expand on that point. I think it's more powerful to leave it hanging. The attitude you choose doesn't only have the power to make or break your day, it also affects those closest to you. That, gorgeous thing, is true Girl Power. Please wield it with the greatest of care.

FACT:
You can't change other people; you can only offer guidance, and lead by example

But there's one more point that needs hammering. I promised I'd tell you how to do your bit for humanity, so please adopt the brace position.

Your 'emotional spillage' creates a ripple effect that reaches three degrees of people removed from you. Meaning you are affecting your friends, your friends' friends, and your friends' friends' friends.

Here are the important numbers: 16, 10 and 6.

Imagine you've got a smile on your face and a positive attitude. Everyone you come into direct contact with experiences an emotional uplift of 16%. Family, friends, teachers. You, on a good day, light up those closest to you by a minimum of 16%.

But it doesn't stop there.

Those 16% happier folk then pass on their happiness to everyone they encounter, raising their levels by 10%. So, for example, your fave teacher is 16% happier because you've had a stellar lesson. She/he goes home to their family and everyone in your teacher's family is now 10% happier (you haven't met your teacher's family, but it's your happiness they've caught).

But there's one more ripple to be rippled. Your teacher's partner pops out to the supermarket to get something for tea and because they're 10% happier, they have some bants with the lady on the self-service checkout and that lady is now 6% happier.

All because *you* were in a good mood to begin with!

How many people do you come into direct contact with every single day? Let me do the sums for you: deliberately guesstimating on the low side, let's assume you meet 3 people at home, 30 other teenagers in class, 5 people at lunch, a lady on the checkout and 5 random passers-by on the way home from school.

That's 44 people that you've come into direct contact with, but remember, the ripple effect reaches three degrees of people removed from you. So your first ripple has reached 44 people.

For the sake of simplicity, let's assume that the 44 you met also meet 44 people. So your emotional ripple has now reached 44 × 44. The second ripple has now been felt by 1,936 people.

And to complete your impact, let's assume those 1,936 people each interact with 44 others.

You might need to sit down for this next number. You will have had some sort of emotional impact on 85,184 people!

Girl, that ain't no ripple. That's a full-on tidal wave! You are the epicentre of a tsunami of emotion that is felt across your family, school and community. That is Wonder Woman territory – you doing your bit for humanity!

Little note: I'm not trotting out these numbers to pressure you into sticking a stupid grin on your face and *pretending* everything's tickety-boo when it's not. Remember, bad days are inevitable.

I'm telling you about the emotional ripple effect for information only. It might stiffen your resolve. Once you understand how impactful you are, it makes sense to work hard at creating more positive days than negative ones. For the sake of yourself and those around you.

And just to cement the message, there's an academic report that also suggests a happy friend makes you 25% happier, a happy brother or sister raises your happiness by 14% and a happy neighbour raises your happiness by a whopping 34%.

So I'll finish with a call to arms:

Be that friend.
Be that sister.
Be that neighbour.

Most of all, I want to say thank you to my mother who said to me: 'Darling, you can be whatever you want to be as long as you're outrageous.

-Phoebe Waller-Bridge, BAFTA acceptance speech

Chapter 16

BE YOU. IT'S AN AWESOME LOOK

you are perfect -
just the way
you are!

There's so much being said about body positivity-slash-neutrality these days that you probably already know what to expect from this little wedge of the book. You might even be able to write it yourself.

It is brilliant that we're finally being given the message that beauty doesn't come in one shape or size or ability or skin colour. But that message is still being delivered far too quietly. It's barely a whisper. We see the *occasional* real-looking woman on the *occasional* advert. So we're stepping in the right direction. We just need to pick up the pace.

Girls have been comparing themselves to representations of other females forever.

I say 'representations' because that's all they've ever been. Clever illusions created by master magicians working for magazines, papers, film, television and online advertisers.

Media images are messed with in a squillion ways before they're published. They are masterpieces, the result of hours and hours of work, usually by teams of professionals: makeup artists, hairstylists, photographers, lighting technicians and post-production experts. And they've been making us real-life humans feel like we don't measure up for as long as any of us can remember.

Supermodel Cindy Crawford famously once said, *'Even I don't wake up looking like Cindy Crawford.'* When a model can look at a professionally produced picture of herself and feel inadequate, that's *got* to tell us something, right?

We can't *ever* measure up, because. . .

Human eyes don't come that sparkly
Human skin can't be that flawless
Human hair doesn't grow that shiny
Human waists aren't that teeny and
Human legs don't go on for that long!
It's special effects. Wizardry.

We *know* that this goes on, right? It's not exactly headline news that the digitally enhanced girl on the cover of *Cosmo* doesn't look like the real-life girl on the photo shoot.

But pictures of people we know on social media? Well, that's different, isn't it? They're more 'real', aren't they?

Not massively.

A storming majority of women under 40 edit their pics before posting them.[1] But a funny thing goes on in our heads when we scroll – we *forget* that nearly everyone does this! Or, at least, we don't consciously remind ourselves when we're looking at the images.

And because we're tricked into thinking our friends' pictures are somehow more genuine, thoughts like 'I've got to keep up with *her*' or 'I've got to out-pretty *them*' begin to whirl inside our heads.

So we do the same. We pose. . . then we edit. . . then we post. . . then we repeat.

And we never stop to think about how crackers it all is, this world of make-believe.

Ever dreamed of having the eyes of a Disney princess with the nose of a woodland creature? Well, dream no more. There's a filter for that!

Even before the makeup and filters get layered on, most of us know how to position our bodies – and our camera phones – to make us look completely different. We know which angles hide the bits we don't want anyone to see. And we know what to do with our faces to make certain features stand out and others blend into the background. We can even default our phones to a special mode that instantly removes our 'flaws' without us having to click a thing. The app version of airbrushing. . . our very own form of wizardry.

---

[1] *The statistics change depending on where you do your research, but it's nearly always above 70%.*

And we're all doing it. *You* are. *She* is. *I* am. I might not use distortion filters or app myself into an animal, but I definitely vet pictures before I post them and choose the ones that show me in the best light.

I've struggled to find the right words for this next bit, so please bear with me. The first time I was even conscious of my weight was when I was three.

THREE!

The doctor made a comment to me in front of my dad. And because of the way he said it, I immediately felt ashamed. In that moment, I suddenly knew what it meant to be 'fat' or 'thin'.

See, apart from when I was born the smallest of twins (not much over five pounds), I have always been an above-average weight. I've always been super-sporty too. . . but my curves showed up early and unless I eat only dust and live at the gym for months of Sundays, my rounded bits tend to stick around.

I cannot say this seriously enough: I ADORE my curves. And I've found, as I've gone through life, other people have adored them, too.

But that hasn't always been the case. I can still recall every single time I've been teased about my body. I felt so bad about myself in my early teens that I developed serious eating issues that stayed with me well into adulthood. And I truly believe they lingered so long because I didn't talk to anyone about them.

And because I didn't talk to anyone about them, no one could clue me up on what I was going through. No one could tell me that it was very common and very human and not at all my fault. That it was my mind's way of coping with the messages I was being given about body image. About how wrong I was getting it. That it was my way of desperately trying to hold onto some control when I was being told that I had none.

And that, with a bit of help, I could come through it wiser, healthier. . . and having found my Fierce.

If you think you might be going through something similar, please know that:

- I'm so proud of you for acknowledging it, even if it was just in your head when you read that last sentence. That really is one of the toughest – and most positive – steps you can take.
- *You* are not your eating problem. You're not an 'anorexic' or a 'bulimic' or any other label. You are an absolutely magnificent human being, going through an especially tough time. The eating problem is not worthy of you and you can look forward to kicking its sorry butt as soon as you get the right support.
- Reaching out for that support will shine the biggest light on what, right now, probably feels like a horribly dark corner in your mind. Talking shrinks the problem a little more each time you do it. Speak to someone you trust first if you want, but if you visit www.fearlessgirls.co.uk, you'll find a list of incredible organisations just waiting to lend their ears, hold your hand and help you find *you* again.
- I believe in *you*. I know it can feel like you're climbing uphill only to come tumbling back down again and again, but you have EVERYTHING you need inside of you to make the final climb. And you will. In the meantime, I'm sending you all the love in the world. Wrap yourself up in it. Then, when you're ready, you can knock the whole ordeal into the next millennium.

My problem was at the larger end of the scale, but for some girls the worry is at the other end. Because, try as they blinkin' well might, they simply cannot *gain* weight. 'The lucky few', you might say. . . but, no. . . rest assured, they get served up their portions of grief.

It's not exactly a new phenomenon. Long before the invention of camera phones, *ye olde worlde* rich folk loved self-portraits because a) they were a mark of status and b) they could control the way they looked in them. The Lord or Lady would get togged up in their finest outfit and pose while the professional went about the portrait. Imagine posing for a five-day selfie! Even in those days the artists had worked out that they needed to show the Lord/Lady in their best light or they'd never work again.

Three, four, five hundred years on, I guess you could say not much has changed. . . other than in ye *olde worlde* days, airbrushing was done with an actual brush.

It all comes back to that addictive drug called 'external validation' and the truth from several chapters ago – if we were full up with love for ourselves, we wouldn't feel so desperate to be validated by the outside world.

I know, I know. I can already hear some of you telling me to 'bore off' as I type. And I get it. Filtering, posing, pouting, editing, airbrushing. . . it's just a bit of fun, right?

On the surface, it may seem that way.

But every time you take a snap of yourself and immediately edit it, you are giving your brain a very powerful message:

'Before you show yourself to ANYONE, you must change. Improve. Upgrade. Do whatever it takes: crop, filter, play with the light. . . turn yourself into a chuffin' reindeer if you have to. Just do NOT look like you. Because you are not good enough as you are.'

That 'harmless fun' is wrecking your self-esteem.

It just so happens that celebrating our imperfections as a thing of beauty would be a game changer.

Earlier, I introduced the Japanese concept of Kintsugi. Something so powerful, it's worth revising. Kintsugi, if you recall, treats breakages as part of the history of an object, rather than something to hide. Apply it to humans and you get the notion that we're all a little bit broken, but what broke you has made you who you are.

Here's Kintsugi's equally powerful sister concept, *wabi-sabi*, which is based around three simple realities: nothing lasts, nothing is finished, and nothing is perfect.

Quirks, anomalies, uniqueness.

You are wabi-sabi. I am wabi-sabi. Everyone is wabi-sabi. Human beings, beautifully crafted by wear and tear.

Revel in your imperfections. The wobbly boobs, the mole, the slightly wonky teeth, the imperfect skin: they make you. . . *you*.

You are just like everyone else, flawed beauty.

Our bodies exist in the *real* world (where we grow, go through puberty, fall down, get bruises and scars, get older, etc.), but our heads exist in a picture-perfect *virtual* world (where none of those things happen).

So when you experience something COMPLETELY NORMAL – like problem skin, weight gain, weight loss, stretch marks, hair growth, hair loss, body odour, weird-looking lady bits, one boob growing differently to the other (or both growing too much. . . or neither growing enough!) – you somehow feel anything BUT normal. . . because everyone else in that virtual, picture-perfect world is still walking around virtually picture-perfect.

Absolutely no one is in the wrong for posting edited pics. It's just the way things are right now. It's the way people want to show up and be seen.

I'm not saying don't read magazines or beauty blogs and don't scroll through other people's pics on social media. What I *will* ask you to do is try these steps the next time you see a seemingly flawless face or body in a seemingly flawless picture and feel like yours might not compare:

1. Remind yourself that the image will have gone through a manufacturing process. It's been built. It's not real.
2. If it's a pic on social media, remind yourself that the person who posted it is in the exact same boat as you – just trying to keep up with everyone else. Send them love in whatever way you can (whether it's a friendly comment or just a friendly thought inside your head).
3. Ask yourself, 'Does this picture make me feel better or worse?' If the answer is 'worse', turn the page, change the channel, put down the device.

You and your time are so precious. Looking at something that makes you feel sad or worried or bad about yourself just doesn't deserve to come high on your list of things to do. Especially when there are so many things out there that'll make you feel fantastic. Top advice: go after those instead.

The thing that makes you most attractive is what you radiate. It's your energy. Which isn't something you can wear or paint on. If you light yourself up with just enough gorgeousness on the inside, it'll shine through you for everyone in the room to see.

Please, please understand how PERFECT you are, just as you are. You don't NEED to buy a product to change the colour of your skin. You don't NEED to buy a stretchy-sticky-Spanxy-type thing that cinches in your waist. You don't NEED to buy shoes that punish your feet just because they make you look a few inches taller. If you WANT to do those things, that's absolutely grand. Crack on cracking on. Just remember that dressing up is supposed to make you feel one thing and one thing only: great. If it doesn't, you're in the wrong clobber. Wear what feels right for *you*, not what looks good on your mate, Mia.

There's nothing I would love more than to tell you that because you've read this book, you will never have a bad thought about your body again. But, sadly, that would be a big, hairy fib. You know now that being human flavour means you'll have good and bad thoughts that'll lead to good and bad feelings, and that's just the wonderful way it is. But you'll also know that when you're having one of 'those days', there will be something you can do to give yourself *better* thoughts that'll get you to *better* feelings. Here are a few suggestions.

1. Give a little respect

When you're feeling bad about your body, sometimes the jump to LOVING it can just feel too big. 'Body neutrality', on the other hand, is more about acceptance, without the pressure of having to adore what you see in the mirror. You know what? You don't have to love *or* hate your body. Instead, you can respect it for what it is (your home) and what it does for you (breathe, get you from A to B, etc.). Tune into what you're proud and thankful for. . . and the love might come later. Or it might not. Either is completely okay.

2. Look at the whole package

If I stood in the mirror poking and pulling at all of my flaws, I would be there a looooong time and I'd walk away feeling horrible. Straight up, I can list five parts of my body that I wouldn't change. . . and about 55 things that, given the option, I would. Instead, when I look in the mirror, I look at the whole of me. And rather than homing in on what I don't like, I focus twice as hard on the things I do. So, try looking at yourself in a 'long shot' and admire the whole package rather than scrutinising individual parts of you, super-close up.

3. Remember, you're not a number

A number on a scale doesn't tell you who you are or what you're worth. It's easy to fall into an obsession with weighing yourself, but it can sometimes create mental obstacles that do more harm than good. And it isn't always a reliable way of monitoring your health, as weight can fluctuate day to day. If your scale makes you feel anxious or lousy, it has too much power over your happiness – throw it out and go by how you feel instead.

4. Put a plan in place

While I don't go on missions to get thin anymore, I do notice when I'm feeling unhealthy and not like *me*. Whenever I reach that place, I make sure I do something about it. Just the act of writing a healthy eating or exercise plan makes me feel so much better. Even on Day One – long before I feel any results – I'm in a more positive frame of mind, simply because I've started to take action. I'm back in control. I know the changes will come and I start to look forward to getting into certain clothes again or reaching a specific level of fitness. It's the NOT doing anything that makes you feel like poo. So, if you're not feeling as good as you know you can feel, there are hundreds of free fitness and nutrition plans online for the pinching. Grab whatever you think will work best for you and make 'One Day' 'Day One'.

5. Set goals for how you feel, not how you look

Exercise and healthy eating are the best things you can do for your body. . . but focus on making it stronger for YOU rather than more attractive for someone else. That's way more empowering.

6. Learn to take a compliment

We remember the negative more than the positive, don't we? Apparently, it takes around 10 compliments to cancel out one negative comment. So when someone says something kind, be sure to bank that baby! We tend to feel the need to throw compliments back at people, for fear of seeming arrogant or big-headed if we accept them. But that couldn't be further from the truth. A compliment is a gift that someone's plucked up the courage to give you. Can you imagine if that same person gave you an actual present, like a piece of jewellery, and you told them it was cheap and tacky, threw it on the floor and stamped on it? That's what you'd be doing by rejecting a compliment from them. So make them feel good with a simple 'thank you'. As long as it's said from a genuine place, it's the most self-assured and gracious response you can give. And you'll both walk away with a lil' spring in your step.

7. Bring back smiling!

A smile is the most beautiful thing you will ever wear. So wear one, a lot. At the risk of sounding ancient, too many smiles seem to have been replaced by pouts these days, and oh, how I miss 'em! Please let's bring them back. Shove one on your face as often as you can. It will instantly lift your mood. . . and do the same for everyone around you.

8. Surround yourself with good vibes

Some people keep uplifting quotes or posters in places they'll see them often. Personally, I like this one:

Just in case no one tells you today:

hello

⸘GOOD MORNING⸘

you're awesome

I believe in you

nice bum

I'll give you that one for nothing. Maybe stick it next to your bedroom mirror.

9. And (altogether now). . . stop comparing!

Look around you! Anyone of any size, any shape, any gender, any ethnicity, any ability, any sexuality, any ANYTHING can look fierce. Show up the way YOU want. There's a chance that the thing you call an 'imperfection' is the one thing that someone else wishes they had. Embrace yourself. . . and have a rollicking good time for as many of your days as possible, without giving too much of a stuff about what anyone else thinks.

You don't need to live up to a make-believe idea of 'perfection'.

Be YOU. It's an awesome look.

I saw a guy at Starbucks today.

No iPhone.

No tablet.

No laptop.

He just sat there.

Drinking coffee.

Like a psychopath.

-Unknown

Chapter 17

HOW TO BE A CLASS ACT ONLINE

it's in your hands

You're young. There's a strong possibility that you're more tech savvy than me. You know more about online than me. You have more followers than I do. You are fluent in emoji. You can double thumb, double fast. You know your home wi-fi password off by heart.

So it's fair to ask, who the chuff am I to tell you anything about how to act online?

Fret not. Before you dive into this chapter, here's a quick Q&A to put your mind at ease:

Q: Are you going to nag me about always being on my phone, like my mum does?
A: Nope. I'm not your mother.
Q: Are you going to tell me to stop using my phone?
A: Don't be ridiculous. I know that's never going to happen.
Q: Are you going to tell me stuff I already know?
A: Perhaps. I'm certainly going to be 'reminding' you of some things you conveniently forget.
Q: Are you going to be all preachy, like, 'It was better back in the olden days when we used to climb trees, build dens and die of rickets'?
A: By now, I'm hoping you'll have figured this book isn't preachy. It's more 'proddy'. [Note to self: proddy isn't a word but it should be.] I'm keen to offer you an alternative angle, some advice or a new way of thinking that will point you in a better direction. It's also worth pointing out that 'knowing' and 'doing' are not the same thing. The motivation to change has to come from you.

So I'll chuck some facts at you and you can do whatever you like with the information.

Fact 1: You are the first generation to have been born into a world where www is established. You were born scrolling, swiping and liking. Your generation is basically a massive social experiment.

Fact 2: You're not going to grow out of your scrolling habit. If anything, you're likely to grow further into it. This isn't *necessarily* a problem, because. . .

Fact 3: The web and social media have provided a platform for some pretty spectacular things, not least having all the information, ever, in the history of the world, available from a small device you carry around with you. That is beyond amazing. It's no wonder you look at it a lot!

Then there's connection: texting your dad, Skyping your gran, FaceTiming your bestie. Again, amazing.

Not to mention that the internet is great at giving people a voice,[1] showcasing talent, promoting events, promoting businesses, spreading good news stories and uplifting content, networking and finding jobs, fundraising, *blah blah blah*.

Basically, new tech has arrived very quickly and on the whole, it's completely epic. Used well, wi-fi is even better than whatever was the best thing *before* sliced bread.

Fact 4: The *problem* with the world wide web is entanglement. It's worth pointing out something blindingly obvious: click-bait is waiting, cheddar ready, to snare you. Tracking technology infiltrates your laptop and phone. In a supreme internet irony, the Slimming World's website has cookies.

Fact 5: Free content is never really 'free'. It's consuming your attention. Your attention is time. And time is all you've got. When you log onto social media and nibble the cheesy click-bait and you're snared for 90 minutes, falling deeper into the never-ending rabbit hole of nonsense, it isn't time out from your actual life. The clock isn't paused. Your 4000 weeks aren't held in suspended animation while you absorb the trivia.

These minutes are your life!

You can't announce, *Okay, I'm clicking pause while I crack on with my social media. I'm gonna check my usual webpages, then Tweets, then*

---

[1] *Depending on what's being shouted, this can also fall into the not-so-good category.*

scroll on FB and 'like' a couple of Instagram stories. Then when I've done all that, I'll resume my life.

Sadly, it doesn't work like that. When you've done all the above, you'll resume your life alright, but it'll be 90 minutes shorter.

The realisation is this: how you spend your minutes adds up to the sum total of how you spend your life.

Fact 6: Research suggests that people of all ages are getting drawn into spending more and more time at a screen. Your generation isn't Gen X, Y or Z. You're not 'millennials'. You're not 'snowflakes'. You're 'screenagers'.

Everything has what's called an 'opportunity cost', which is *basically the next best thing that you could have been doing*. If, as surveys suggest, young people are spending 9 hours a day on the internet (which incidentally is more time than you spend sleeping), then by age 80 you will have clocked up 30 solid years of screen time.

Three whole decades. That's a lot of cat videos!

Apart from being a sobering thought, that also carries a massive opportunity cost. It's 30 years that you could have spent making eye contact with real people, chatting to flesh-and-blood friends, eating ice creams, walking in the drizzle, watching sunsets, learning to play the piano, working towards your ambitions, or, indeed, stroking a real cat.

Fact 7: There's been a measurable rise in self-interest (the posh word is narcissism) as well as a race to get more followers and the desire to be famous for the sake of being famous. Once these patterns are grooved into your mind, they're very difficult to shake off.

Like I said, those are the facts. Do with them what you will.

In terms of taking positive action, it's hard not to laugh at the official advice for smartphone detoxing, which is to download an app that tells you how long you've been on the phone.

Sorry, come again? Download an app?

To *detox* your phone addiction, you *download an app. To your actual phone?*

I mean, the world's gone billy bonkers, surely?

That's like detoxing an alcoholic with a bottle of gin or curing obesity with a 12-inch deep-pan pepperoni with stuffed crusts and extra cheese. And ice cream.

Here's my basic smartphone advice, take it or leave it. Basically, to wrestle back control, everything you do on your phone should be *intentional*. That means:

- Signing out of each app after you've used it. This will require you to sign back in every time, which is too much hassle, plus there's not much chance you'll remember the password, so you can't just mindlessly open your apps whenever you have a free second.
- Even better, deleting all social media apps from your phone; check these only from a desktop computer. *It's likely you've just freaked out/rolled your eyes at the thought of this one. And I get it, I really do. It's just a suggestion. That works. It'll make you feel a hell of a lot calmer if you suspect the balance has tipped too far in the wrong direction.
- Turning all banner-style/pop-up/sound notifications *off*. Yep, ALL of them. It puts you in charge of your phone instead of your phone bossing you.
- Leaving your phone in your pocket or keeping it out of sight at school, get-togethers, during conversations and meals. No, not face down, *out of sight*. That leaves you free to focus 100% on the people in the room.
- Keeping your phone out of sight on your way to and from school. Chat. Watch the world go by instead. You'll see lots of people on their phones. Smile at the irony.

- NOT texting on the toilet. For no reason, other than it's gross.
- Choosing two hours a day to switch off your phone. And then sticking to it.
- Instead of thinking about 'spending less time on your phone', thinking about 'spending more time on your life'.

When online, the key thing to remember is that your digital footprint lasts forever. I mean, *forever* forever.

With every tap and every click, you're building up a picture of who you are and how you want to be seen. Even when you hit 'delete', none of it ever really disappears. It stays in the ether and is always find-able. So you've got to get good at being your own PR agent. Before posting anything, assume it'll be seen by the world and his guinea pig.

If you think of your life as a movie, then your digital footprint is the trailer. Just like people glance at trailers to get the gist of a movie, they'll glance at your profile to get the gist of you. New friends, future partners, the admissions department of the uni you're applying to, prospective employers. . . many of them will look at your digital 'reel' before deciding whether to invest any more of their time and energy in the real thing. Even if you could charm the birds out of the trees in person, you won't get the chance if your online presence isn't impeccable. In other words, this stuff matters.

> *Never worry what cool people think.*
> *Head for the warm people.*
> *Life is warmth.*
> *You'll be cool when you're dead.*
> Matt Haig

Before posting anything, it's a good idea to pause for a minute and question your intention. Is it positive or negative? There is a huge difference between speaking up *with intention* and speaking up *for attention*.

Dropping hints in public posts ('People can be SO rude' and the like) will do way more harm than good. True assertiveness and class would be telling the person in question how you feel, rather than posting sentences, quotes or lyrics that only hint at it.

And just like in the real world, it's never okay to be cruel. Cruelty can and does pick up a LOT of momentum online. No one should have to suffer being attacked by an army of keyboard warriors who are blind to the damage they're doing. You never know what battle a person might be fighting and just how far a single comment could tip them over the edge. Compassion is always the way to go. Always.

If you suspect your intention might be of the negative variety, put the device down and let the urge ride itself out. Just like waves rise up and come crashing back down, the urge to post something destructive will lose its momentum if you just give it a moment. Then you'll be able to think more clearly and post in a way that your future self will thank you for.

Social is here to stay. But the device will always be in YOUR hands. It doesn't have the power to creep its way into more of your life than you want it to. The trick is to get the best from IT, rather than letting IT take the best from YOU. To be its master, not its slave. So here are a few guidelines, from me to you. For no other reason than I love you, wholeheartedly:

1. Think of online space as real-life space. If you wouldn't let strangers into your home, don't let them into your profile. All accounts come with privacy settings – make sure yours are set to block people you don't know. That way, you'll stay in control of who sees your stuff.
2. Remember that not everything is as it seems. There are lots of brilliant people out there, but there's the odd shady character hanging about, too. Keep in mind that anyone can set up a social media profile using someone else's pics and info, and don't agree to meet someone you

don't know offline. Unless they're hot in their profile pic. I'm joking. Of *course* I'm joking! NEVER meet someone you don't know offline, full stop.

3. If anything feels scary, make some noise. Just like IRL, no one should be making you uncomfortable online. If you're being harassed or intimidated, take screenshots. Talk to someone you trust or an organisation like the Cybersmile Foundation, which will give you the support you need. You can also shout out to the social media platform it's happening on, using their reporting function. Again, just like IRL, you never have to face anything alone.

4. Be prepared for some delightful acts of chivalry. I hope you sensed the irony in that last sentence. As a female, it's likely, at some point, that someone somewhere will think it perfectly okay to send you a pic of themselves in the 'altogether'. In other words, they might send you more than you want to see. If you feel happiest hitting 'delete', go ahead. If you need to talk to someone about it, then that's what you should do. But if you'd rather push back, something that's worked for me in the past has been to reply with 'No thanks' and a sea of sad faces ☹ ☹ ☹ ☹ (nobody wants this response to a snap of their yoo-hoo. And it might just make them think twice before doing it again).

> FACT:
> Just because you can doesn't mean you should

5. Never ever feel *pressured* to pose (in your 'altogether'). A lot of this is about knowing your own gut. But standing your ground is hard to do when there's pressure to please someone else. Especially if you *like* that someone else! Giving into the pressure can make you feel insecure and anxious, because you can never be sure that what you share will stay with the person it's intended for, and that can leave you feeling a little freaked. Above all, remember this: the way a guy

or girl treats you online is a good indication of how they'll treat you offline. So ask yourself, 'Do I want to get into anything with someone who keeps pushing me to do something I'm not comfortable with?' You can be assertive but non-aggressive with replies like:

'Sharing stuff like that has never worked out well for anyone I know. So I'm gonna pass for now.'

Or

'I'm sure you'd keep them private, but the internet might not.'

If their response isn't respectful, chances are they're the type of person who'd share pictures without your consent and you'll have avoided a nightmare situation.[2]

6. Remember, it's called *social* media, so keep it nice and uplifting. Don't ever post antisocial stuff. There's just no need. The general rule is that if you haven't got anything nice to post. . . don't post.

7. It's the same rule with trolls and haters. If they have a go at you (which at some point they will), either ignore them or kill them with kindness. I recently spotted one of my social media heroines doing this brilliantly. Here's how the chat went:

Troll: You are so CREEPY AND CRINGY! (barfing emojis)

Kristina Kuzmic: Oh man. I don't think it's healthy for you to see my posts since they cause such an extreme, negative reaction. Here are instructions on how to block my page. Wishing you all the best!

a. Go to the page you want to block.
b. Click ⋯ below the Page's cover photo.
c. Select **Block Page**.
d. Click **Confirm**.

I mean. . . just. . .

Remember, trolls live under bridges. Bridges are dark places, their lives must be horrible. And haters hate everyone, especially themselves.

Never become one of them.

---

[2] *Don't panic if any of this has already happened. You won't find a person on the planet who hasn't done stuff in the past that they now regret. The way forward is to accept you've made choices that can't be erased but that you can create a better footprint from this day forward. . . ones that are reflective of who you really are.*

8. When someone does land an online blow, be prepared by doing
   this activity:
   In the postage stamp box below, write the names of people you
   know and truly respect. The box is deliberately small because there
   won't be many. Your gran, stepdad, a teacher or two, your best
   friend, maybe your big sis.
   And when the online mud has been slung and it's hit you slap in the
   face, have a look at the names in the box. Remember, these are the
   people whose opinions you truly value and trust. Is the name of the
   mud-slinger in that box?

   I'm guessing not.
   In which case, whatever they've slung doesn't actually matter.
   Move on.
9. Be an Upstander, not a Bystander. If you see someone else taking a
   bullet online, stick up for them. Neutralise a mean comment with a
   gorgeous one. If someone's getting hateful messages, get in touch
   and check they're okay. Don't let hate survive on your watch, missus.
   Go on a mish to make the online world a better place.

FACT:
We sometimes do things that
are permanently foolish just
because we are temporarily
upset

10. And finally, if something makes you feel uncomfortable or rubbish, if deep down in your gut it doesn't feel right, close it down. Give your eyes and fingers a break from it. For as long as necessary. And if you feel the need, talk to someone about it. Remember, you have control over what you consume. Always.

    So, it's kind of the same deal online as in real life, isn't it? Aim to light up the screen in precisely the same way you'd want to light up a room.

    Because that, lovely, is class!

I was always pretty ambitious... I remember my mum once said, 'I suppose you'll give it a year and see if you can make it as an actress?' And I said, 'No Mum, I think I'll give it 10.'

-Olivia Colman

Chapter 18

HOW TO NEVER DO A DAY'S WORK IN YOUR LIFE

Think of this as a bonus chapter. I'm not just prodding you to make good decisions NOW, I'm attempting to set you up for life. One day – and it'll happen quicker than you think – you'll enter the big wide world of work.

So here's your heads-up: work is called 'work' for a reason. You can dress it up how you like, but the bare-faced truth is that it involves you giving up about a third of your life, in return for money. Someone has to pay you to do it. If they didn't pay you, you most definitely *wouldn't* do it. For the vast majority, work is something they'd prefer NOT to do. It's to be endured, not enjoyed.

But you don't have to be part of the 'vast majority'. This is another of those occasions when it pays to be in the minority.

When pondering your future, it's worth considering the differences between a job, a career and a calling.

If you're doing a 'job', you'll feel it in the pit of your stomach. Going to work will be a chore. You'll be doing it because it pays the bills and you'll get that feeling of angst when the alarm goes off at stupid o'clock.

Next level is a 'career'. It's a bit like a job but there will be opportunities for advancement. The money's not stellar to start with, but there's progression. It's up the evolutionary scale from a 'job' and you're likely to feel you're moving in the right direction. If you've got a career, you're more likely to be interested in your work and want to do well. Whoever employs you is likely to invest in some training – because you're worth it.

Thought for the day:
You don't get what you wish for, you get what you work for.

A 'calling' is where you feel fulfilled and have a sense of contribution to the greater good. Your 'work' is likely to draw on your personal strengths and give your life meaning and purpose. I put 'work' in inverted commas because it *is* work but it won't *feel* like work. If you're employed in your calling, you'll feel totally alive and you'll love what you do. The pay may be good or it may be bad. Either way, money's not the point because – whisper it – *whatever it is you're doing, you'd probably do it for free.*

Here's the interesting part. Whether you're engaged in a job, career or calling has less to do with your work than you might imagine. A 'calling' can have just as much to do with your mindset as it does with the actual work being done. There's a classic example from way back, when President John F. Kennedy was visiting NASA's headquarters for the first time in 1961. While touring the rocket facility, he introduced himself to a janitor who was mopping the floor and asked him what he did at NASA.

'I'm helping put a man on the moon!'

In his case, sweeping the floor (which may seem like a job to you or me) was his calling. The man had purpose.

This links with Simon Sinek's amazingly simple concept of the 'Golden Circle'. His model is represented below.

For the record, most adults start at the outside of the circle and work inwards. So, for example, I'd expect your mum/dad/gran to know *what* their job is. Go ahead and ask them. They'll say things like 'I'm a teacher' [carer, nurse, administrator, carpet seller, shelf stacker, brain surgeon, nail technician, stay-at-home mum, sales rep, engineer, checkout operator, accountant, astronaut, MI5 agent, whatever].

Basically, everyone will know WHAT their job is.

Back to Sinek's Golden Circle. Most people can also answer the *'how'* question. Your mum will know *what* she does and *how* she does it. For example, if the WHAT is *'I'm a teacher'*, the HOW might be *'I deliver science to ages 12–18'*.

But the middle bit is crucial. It also happens to be the hardest question to answer. *WHY* do you do what you do? *WHY* do you get out of bed in the morning? *WHY* do you go to work? *WHY* do you deliver science to teenagers?

The honest answer to that question, for most people, is *because I have to*. Or, *because it pays the bills*.

And hey presto, they will be doing a 'job' or a 'career'. Forty-five years of low-level drudgery, muddling along for the pay, counting down to the weekend, accidentally wishing their life away.

To maintain maximum motivation, you need to find a clear and compelling WHY. You need an inspiring reason to get out of bed. In short, you need a purpose.

> *When you live*
> *life connected to*
> *purpose, you don't*
> *have to chase*
> *opportunities, they*
> *come to you.*
>
> Sue Fitzmaurice

Simon Sinek weaves a compelling argument that the majority of great people, the people who have made a real difference in the world, started with a compelling 'why'. But the good news is that you don't have to be Catherine the Great, Mother Teresa or Rosa Parks to make a difference.

You, living your best life, will do just fine.

Finding and following your WHY is like rocket fuel.

If you're struggling to get out of bed on a dark Monday morning, the chances are you need to find your why. So let's have a go at WHAT/HOW/WHY, but in a school context.

I'm going to work it the *wrong* way first and work from the outside-in, which is what most people do.

WHAT do you do?
I go to school five days a week.
HOW do you do that?
I attend lessons, take some notes, learn some stuff, have lunch, learn some more stuff, and go home.
WHY do you go to school?
Because everyone else does. I have to. I think it's the law?

That wishy-washy WHY is why most teenagers slouch their way into school on Monday morning and skip out at 3.30 on Friday.

The rocket fuel comes when you *start* with your WHY. Get that nailed and the HOW and WHAT tend to look after themselves.

So let's go again, this time from the inside-out.

WHY do you go to school?

I go to school because it's a fabulous opportunity to set me up for the rest of my life.

HOW do you do that?

I listen, learn, absorb and take part. I'm the best learner I can be.

WHAT do you do?

I invest in my future, five days a week.

BOOM! We have lift-off!

If you're struggling with your motivation, it's helpful to have a think about the next 3000 weeks of your life and ask yourself this question: *What's my sentence?*

So, if there was one sentence that would sum you up for the rest of your life, what would that sentence be?

One *magnificent* sentence!

It could be anything from 'She's an amazing human being who always does her very best' to 'She's an inspiration to family and friends' to 'Someone who makes good things happen' to 'A doer of good deeds' to 'A person who makes a difference'.

If you can sum yourself up in one fabulous sentence, you'll find it's also your WHY.

So when your mojo is slipping and the world is conspiring against you, remember your sentence, be that version of you, and you'll be back in the game.

Best of all, you'll never have to do a day's 'work' in your life.

Your Sentence:

_____
_____
_____
_____
_____
_____
_____
_____
_____
_____
_____
_____
_____
_____
_____
_____
_____
_____

Listen to the MUSTN'Ts, child
Listen to the DON'Ts
Listen to the SHOULDN'Ts
The IMPOSSIBLES,
the WON'Ts
Listen to the NEVER HAVES
Then listen close to me:
Anything can happen, child,
ANYTHING can be.

SHEL SILVERSTEIN

Chapter 19

THE GREATEST
STORY EVER TOLD

I'm gonna finish with a story.

It's the best story ever told. But it's a bit different.

You know how stories have a beginning, middle and end. . .

. . . in that order?

Forget that. This one doesn't. I think the whole beginning/middle/end thing has become a bit dated. In *Girl's Guide* Chapters 1–18 I've been banging on about daring to be different, taking a risk or two, finding your brave.

How *same old, same old* just ain't working.

So, rather than follow the crowd, I thought I'd set a new trend. Chapter 19 is a story and I'm going to start it at the end.

Yes, in a break from tradition, the *beginning* is the actual *end*.

So your plot spoiler alert, right here right now, is this: *the main character is going to die in the very first sentence.*

I'm warning you now so it's not a shock later.

And that's not even the crazy bit because then, after I've *started* at the end, I'm going to write the *beginning* and stick it in the *middle*.

So the beginning is the middle, and the middle bit, which is usually about halfway, is going to be spliced onto the end, so the final bit is the *middle*.

So it's *end, beginning*, then *middle*. And get this, the plot twist is, therefore, in the *middle* (because, of course, that's the end. Please keep up!).

Before I start at the end, there's something else you need to know. An important detail. The star of our story – the one who dies right at the beginning (which happens in no story ever) – she had a big family. And because she was not only a grandma but a GREAT grandma, that meant she had GREAT grandkids.

It's a weird fact of life that all GREAT grandchildren are little. Actually, I think there should be a government inquiry to investigate why there are no GREAT grandchildren who are 23, or 18. Or 10 even.

While you're working that one out, here's its relevance to this particular story.

Our hero, who's about to be killed off, is a GREAT grandma so, for reasons specified above, she has very young GREAT grandkids. And when you're little you struggle to say 'Great Grandma Joy' so the kids had shortened it, and pretty much everyone else had adopted the abbreviation, 'GGJ'.

That's who Great Grandma Joy ended up being. It became a bit of a thing. 'GGJ' is what she was called and the faster you said it, the funnier it was. Her slightly older grandkids would have competitions to see who could say 'GGJ' the quickest.

I know you'll have just tried.

Okay, back to the story.

More specifically, the END of the story (which, if you remember, is the actual beginning).

The end

GGJ's funeral was packed. Like, jam-packed.

Family and friends had been allowed into the ceremony but it seemed that half the town's folk were milling around outside, waiting to pay their respects. . . and also probably hoping for a free sandwich. An egg one, because they're special.

And maybe a sausage roll.

There were people of all ages in church, and the weird thing was that everyone was wearing bright colours. And I mean super-bright: sun-kissed oranges, in-yer-face yellows, sky-at-night reds and screaming pinks. Grandad Philip had an electric blue suit, fluorescent green tie, red socks and purple trainers.

It was horrible. I mean, a grandad, *in trainers*?

And he was one of the less colourful ones.

You needed shades to look at Aunty Brenda, who, to be fair, had cheated. She was wearing her costume from the town's am dram 'Joseph' production, her Amazing Technicolour Dreamcoat pretty much stealing the show.

My point is this, I promise you, there was absolutely NO black.

Imagine? A funeral with absolutely no black? Or grey even.

Even the preacher had made an effort, wearing her bright red cloaky thing that was usually reserved for royal occasions.

To cut a long ending short, the preacher woman in the red gowny thing told some stories, GGJ's coffin was taken away, and the hangers-on got their free egg sandwich and sausage roll. There were some cheesy scones, too, which were epic.

To be fair, there were some tears. Lots of tears, actually. Just because you wear a bright-coloured dress and scoff a free cheesy scone doesn't automatically make you happy. [Note to self: it does actually help a bit though.]

Funerals are always sad. There's absolutely no 'fun' in a funeral. That's just a fact.

But after the sniffles had been sniffed and a few pints of Guinness had helped the sausage rolls go down, the mood brightened.

Considerably!

There was laughter and smiles. In fact, it all got a bit silly. There were stories told and photos passed round. Nephew Alexander told the story about the time GGJ got chased by a bull and Aunty Violet laughed so much that she had a little accident.

Then there was the one about the charity skydive. There was the family holiday of 1995 and GGJ's 'surfing incident'. There was Bonfire Night 2003 when she made soup for the entire village, the time she accidentally locked herself out of her house wearing her towel, they remembered the first day she ever got to use an iPad and learned how to swipe, the time that Great Grandad Stephen had set her up on an online dating site, just for a laugh, and how so many men had 'liked' her. Obviously, she'd got her own back by setting her husband up on a very rude dating site and noticed how many weirdos had 'liked' him, too.

So, sure, there were tears that GGJ was gone, but a whole lot of love for the value she'd added to everyone's lives. Nobody could recall a cross word. Nobody could remember a grumble (even in the last few days, which had been tough). Everybody could remember kind deeds. Everybody recalled GGJ just 'being there' for them, having time for them, saying nice things about people and, above all, smiling.

GGJ hadn't been a pouter. She hadn't been big on selfies. She'd been a smiler and had taken part in a lot of 'otheries' – that's what she actually called them – pictures of her and others, all with stupid grins on their chops. GGJ wasn't big on looking cool. Instead, she was ABSOLUTELY ENORMOUS on looking happy.

And as the photos were passed around, there was one in particular that I noticed.

It was taken before smartphones had been invented. I think they were called Polaroids or something? It wasn't on a tablet or anything. It was a small square picture taken in GGJ's back garden.

It was GGJ when she was a kid. And I realised in an all-of-a-sudden kind of way that, *oh my gosh*, GGJ's happiness had started way back.

The beginning

Once upon a time there was a little girl called Joy. And, by and large, she was.

Her first five years were exactly like yours and they flashed by in a blur of swashbuckling adventure. By age five, Joy had ticked all the under-five boxes (ask your mum, you'll have ticked these, too): you've eaten at least one worm, pooed in a swimming pool, trapped your fingers in a door, cuddled a cat so hard you nearly killed it, fallen asleep in your pudding, been sick on a bus driver and nearly died from falling down the stairs.

Sometimes these things happen in a single day!

Here's a graph you've never seen anywhere else (because I've only just this minute invented it) which charts 'age' along the bottom and 'percentage of your life spent in play mode' up the side. The downward trajectory is a bit depressing.

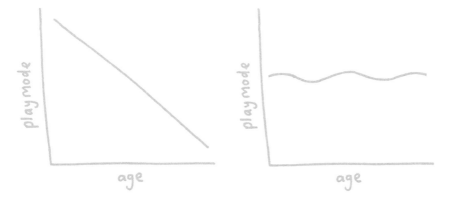

The good news is that 'play mode' is always there. The bad news is that as you get older you accidentally switch into 'teenage mode' or 'work mode' or 'serious mode' or 'angry mode' or 'exhausted mode'. There's a 'can't be bothered mode' that some people default to, too.

It just so happens that Joy's ability to play was ninja level. She had 'work' and 'serious' modes, but she spent a lot of time in 'play'. Her graph was different, a bit like the one on the right.

The result was that whenever you were with Joy, the world just went 'POP'. Trees were greener, skies bluer, puddles puddlier and rainbows rainbowier. There were animals to be spotted in the clouds, including, once, a moose with a hat on. Instead of NOT stepping on the cracks in the pavement, you did the opposite. You could see Joy and her mates a mile off, leaping and bounding to school because they were ONLY allowed to step on the cracks in the pavement. Being with Joy was an ants-in-your-pants experience. Homework was fun. Museums came to life. The library was loud and giggly. Waiting never felt like waiting and being bored never existed. In fact, when you spent time with Joy you were the opposite of bored – which is probably *un*bored or maybe even *de*bored or *anti*-bored.

I'm not quite sure, and neither is Google.

Being in 'play mode' is how we all start out. Remember back to when you were five or eight or something – you were literally the world's best at games, imagination, running, jumping, sand-pitting, drawing, laughing, dressing up, dressing your dog up, paddling in streams, bouncing, giggling, burping, sledging, building dens, skipping, putting your hand up, making up games and climbing? *Especially* climbing! When you're six, you see a climbing frame and it needs conquering.

But you know what? Joy's willingness and ability to play were only part of the story.

She was different in other ways, too. Sure, she was made of 37 trillion cells, just like you and me, but her *habits* were different.

More specifically, her *thinking* was different.

And more specifically than that, there were three things that were radically different.

And even more specifically specific than the previous point that was already specific, two of the three things were things that Joy was doing MORE of and the third was something she was doing LESS of.

Yes, that sentence is a mouthful and I could have simplified it, but I love it!

Here's the number one thing she DID. . .

. . . *she was nice.*

I know, it seems so simple, and if you're reading this book, you (or your mum/dad) have spent a tenner that goes into my Aston Martin fund, so, thank you, you're already 'nice'.

As it happens, most people are nice. I call it 'ordinary nice'. Most folk are kind and considerate, most of the time.

The thing about Joy was that she was nice to everyone, all of the time, even to the not-so-nice. She had nice thoughts about people. She saw the best in everyone. She was genuinely pleased when other people did well, and best of all, she said nice things about people behind their back.

Oh, and in case you're wondering, she wasn't faking it. Joy wasn't *pretending* to be nice and then saying nasty stuff behind people's backs. She was what I call authentic. Proper nice. The real deal.

It doesn't sound a lot, but this upgrade from 'ordinary nice' to 'extraordinary nice' raised her likeability bar. Bottom line, Joy was a joy to be around.

Her niceness leaked.

Joy *radiated* niceness.

I mean, that doesn't sound too taxing, does it?

The second thing that Joy was doing was 'everything'.

Once again, in the interests of simplicity, I don't mean she was *literally* doing everything because nobody can do 'everything'. You'd die of busyness while you made pancakes and surfed at the same time.

Joy lived by a mantra that can be summed up in seven words: *do it better than you have to*.

So everything she did, she did better than she had to.

I've already explained that Joy was nicer than she had to be. But that was only the tip of the big cold thing from Antarctica. Joy used her manners better than she had to. She tried harder than she had to. She put her hand up in class more often than she had to. She was a bit more confident than she had to be. Braver, too. Joy did her homework a bit better than she had to, she ate a bit healthier than she had to and did a little more exercise than she had to.

Joy helped around the house, tidied her room, looked after her guinea pigs, hugged her dad, made people smile, played outdoors, listened, got out of bed on time, went to bed on time, came home from parties on time, Skyped her grandpa, thanked her teachers, read more books, played hockey, ate yukky veggies, played with her annoying little brother, visited her nan, had a positive attitude. . . all *a little bit better than she had to*.

Best of all, she dared to be more fearless than she had to.

And all these little 'better than she had tos' added up to a really big thing that I'm calling 'proper, genuinely, humblingly nice'.

Because, you see, the vast majority *do what they have to* and leave it at that.

It really wasn't a big thing, but it ended up having a big impact.

So, just to revise, the two things Joy was doing that everyone else *wasn't* doing were:

1. Being nice.
2. Doing everything a bit better than she had to.

I suspect there's a saying about rocket science that fits right here?

Which brings me onto the third thing, which, if you recall, was something Joy *wasn't* doing.

Looking down.

She was a looker-upper. And if that isn't a real word, here's another I've just made up: Joy was a noticer.

Which meant she spent way less of her day on *screen time*.

I know, I know. You'll have winced at that.

There's a strong possibility that life without FaceTube, AmazonFlix, InstaBook and an X-Station is your worst nightmare. *Not* sitting for hours scrolling on your tablet may cause a sudden outbreak of cold sweats and the need for actual real doctor tablets. *Not* being able to binge on cartoons might cause a case of 'Cartoon Withdrawal Syndrome'. And imagine the horror if you were never allowed to watch another funny cat video. Your life would be over, right?

To be clear, Joy was doing *a bit* of screen time but an awful lot less than her peers.

Joy once sat on a bench and watched the world go by. Remember, because she was a looker-upper, she wasn't staring down, she was looking around, at passers-by, and she noticed a pattern. A *looking at their screen* pattern.

Joy put her imagination six-pack into action and wondered what human beings would be like in a thousand years from now. No, scrub that. *A million!* She imagined that in a million years from now, when we've evolved a bit more, humans would have huge thumbs, for scrolling. Homo sapiens would have become 'homo scrollions'. Or 'homo swipeans'. Maybe the ability to look upward would have become extinct. We'd heard tales of sky, stars and the moon, but nobody had ever seen them.

Joy was good at noticing. And because she was a noticing ninja, she noticed that she'd noticed something about noticing. She noticed that the longer we stare at our screens, the less we notice.

You're probably thinking, *so what?*

Here's your big, fat SO WHAT: if we charted Joy's early years, you'd find that at age nine, she was epic! But it's easy to be epic at nine. The thing about Joy is that she was still epic at 10, 11 and 12.

Then the clock struck 13 (BONG^{in your head, 13 times}) and it was Teenager O'clock.

Dun dun duuuuun!

Her dad decided she needed a phone. The absolute truth is that she didn't *need* one – she'd thrived for 13 years without one – but everyone else had one so he thought his little girl should have one, too.

There's a technical scientific term for it. Remember from earlier? It's called 'fitting in'.

But despite having a phone, Joy still preferred to look up rather than down. She continued to notice. Sure, she joined a few groups and sometimes texted her mum and Skyped her old folks, but the phone stayed mostly in her bag. So while everyone else on the school bus was glued to their screens (sometimes even the driver, *yikes!*), Joy smiled and noticed and imagineered as she watched the world go by. And at bedtime, when everyone else texted and scrolled through a bad night's sleep, Joy's phone lit up, in her bag, in the kitchen, while she slept soundly.

Joy would wake up refreshed, rejuvenated and excited for the day ahead. That even happened on Mondays, btw.

And this is pretty much how it went. Joy was more interested in actual real people. She connected with them in real life rather than via wi-fi. To be clear, Joy wasn't on zero screen time, just much less than everyone else. So while they got worse at eye contact and real conversation, Joy got better.

Much better.

Much, *much* better.

In fact, over time, there were many more 'muches' added to that sentence. Looking up instead of down created a massive advantage. The gap between Joy's social skills and everyone else's social skills became ginormous.

And then, age 18, Joy left school and the beginning of our story (which is actually the middle) comes to an end.

It's a bit of a sudden end, which makes it exactly like school. One day you're at school and the next day you've left.

The middle bit of your life stretches ahead like a long, winding cul-de-sac with a billion different roads that all lead to the end.

The middle

Now here's the interesting part. This is the middle of the story, but I've shoved it at the end.

And not only is the middle the end, it's also missing. It's a non-middle.

Remember we started with the actual end where GGJ died (God rest her soul and all that) and they all ate cheesy scones?

Then the actual middle bit was the beginning, so way before GGJ became known as GGJ, she was Joy.

The bit between 'Joy' and 'GGJ', the middle bit, that's the part of the story that's missing. That just so happens to be the biggest part and, for me, the best bit.

It's like a jam donut. No, scrap that. It's like one of those *custardy* donuts. No scrap that too, I've never had one, but rumour has it that you can now get salted caramel ones? It's *definitely* like one of those.

My point? There's magic in the middle.

That's the part I want you to think about. The jammy, custardy or salted caramelly bit. And when you've thought about it, I want you to write the best bit of the story.

In fact, I've left you some blank pages so you can do exactly that.

Here's something that should stimulate your thinking, followed by some questions that should stimulate some writing. . .

Fact: the habits that you get into NOW will stick with you forever. Basically, habits become grooved into your brain, which creates the future you. Ultimately, your life isn't about one big decision, it's about thousands of tiny everyday ones. I'd like to think that Joy read *Girl's Guide*, got into a really good groove and stayed in that groove for the entire journey.

Good decisions and great choices – *consistently* – that's the trick.

And that wowza funeral gives you a clue as to the impact she had, not just on her own happiness but on those around her.

Oh, and in case you're wondering, for the record, GGJ never won the lottery, she didn't ever have a Ferrari and she lived in a modest house in a normal street in an average part of town.

Her circumstances weren't extraordinary.

She was.

But you're not GREAT Grandma Joy, or GGJ, or Joy. You're you.

You have total freedom of choice. I totally get that. *Girl's Guide* was written to nudge you towards making some really good choices that groove you into being an amazing human being, which, spookily enough, will determine how your life turns out.

It bugs me that teachers and parents keep asking you the wrong question – a lazy question – which is this: *'What do you want to be when you grow up?'*

I'd like to finish this book with a much better question, which is this: *'What* <u>kind of person</u> *do you want to be when you grow up?'*

I'm pretty sure you already know the answer, so here's a slightly weird activity that will get you to reveal it.

Summoning your very best imagination (the one you had when you were eight), I'd like you to project yourself to the end.

'The end' being a funeral, a bit like GGJ's.

Except it's not GGJ's.

It's yours.

[Gulp!]

Relax, yours is a long way off. But imagine. . .

. . . the place of worship is crammed. Standing room only. The colours are vibrant and, yes, there are people milling around expecting a sausage roll and hoping for a free cheesy scone.

If that's the *end* of your life, I'd like you to use the blank pages at the end of this chapter titled "The Story of My Life" to reflect the lessons from *Girl's Guide* and write the middle bit.

The story.

YOUR story.

The salted caramelly bit.

In fact, let's call it 'The Story of Your Life', turn it into a movie and stick it on at the cinema.

Anything goes.

Please note, this isn't some depressing story about dying. From the moment we're born, we're destined to die, and I'm well aware that there's no such thing as a happy ending. Not where life's concerned. Nowhere in the universe is there a single gravestone that reads *'She Loved Everything About Her Life, Especially the Dying Bit at the End'*.

I'm not asking you to write about a bang-average life where nothing happened.

I'm asking you to write about a life – YOUR life – that ends in full colour. And to, therefore, think about what would have to happen for it to end in full colour.

Remember, this book is called 'A Girl's Guide to Being Fearless'. It's NOT called 'A Girl's Guide to Reading the Book and Then Not Being Bothered to Do the Final Epic Activity'.

So here goes!

These questions might prompt some thinking and hopefully some writing. Or they might not. They're random. You don't have to stick to them, but they might help you write 'The Story of Your Life'.

Your *best* life.

- Gosh, there are so many people at my funeral. And they're all wearing such bright colours. Family, friends, neighbours. . . why are there so many? Surely it can't just be a free egg sandwich and the chance of there being some cheesy scones?
- What kind of habits served me well?
- What kind of attitude did I have, towards learning, teachers, family and life?
- What was I like at 15? What did I need to change at 15?
- What kind of friend was I?
- What kind of daughter was I?
- How did I respond when life got tough (which it did, several times)?
- What did my teachers say about me at school?
- What did I achieve?
- What kind of job(s) did I do? How many jobs did I have? Oh, and what was I like to work with?
- How hard did I work?
- What kind of things did I say, and do? And think? That last one's important! For my life to have been so amazing, what thoughts were going through my head?
- What happened after I left school? Did that full-colour me go to uni or college or get an apprenticeship?
- Who did I fall in love with, and why did I fall in love with them?
- And why did they fall in love back?
- What kind of learner was I?
- What did I say 'yes' to?
- What did I say 'no' to?
- What kind of parent and grandparent was I?

- What hobbies did I have?
- How happy was I?
- What qualities did I have?
- What things did I have to stop doing?
- What small changes had the biggest impact on my life?

THE STORY OF MY LIFE

THE END...

or perhaps a brand
:NEW: beginning?

That, darling reader, is entirely up to you
x

Acknowledgements

The hugest of THANK YOUs to:

Graeme. The other pea in my pod. Thanks for staying solid when I go all squiggly. And for solo parenting so I could get this thing done. You astonish me and I love you.

Mum. For the unwavering support and for never telling me to get a 'proper job'. And for the waffle. . . sorry, wisdom.

Dad. For making me fall in love with language. I hope I'm making you proud, sat up on that cloud somewhere.

My big sisters, Carol and Alex. My first ever 'fearless' female role models.

My twin brother, Paul. We couldn't be more different, but a twin bond never dies.

Andy, Caroline and their respective broods. Jeez, I'm glad we found you.

My nephew, Rhys. The first little boy I ever loved. I hope we find our way back to each other.

Mo and Peter and the extended Lavington/Andrew clan. I love being a part of your family.

Hamish Paton, Emer Lynam and Graeme Campbell. Three awesome bosses who became wonderful friends. I'm beyond grateful for everything you taught me, and I adore your very bones.

Anna West, Melanie Dean and Sarah Dunning. Three of the best mentors and friends a girl could ever hope to have. You are love and bravery personified.

My Fearless Girl tribe: Emily, Soph, Charlotte, Amy, Carly, Nikki, Ceri, Hayley, Mary, Nicola, Katrina, Emma, Katie, Paula, Lorna and the spectacular women I've met in more recent years. You save me.

Angela and Andy next door. Thank you for lending me your attic. It meant I could write for a full hour at a time without hearing the word 'mummy'. Priceless.

Andy Whittaker. For giving me the nudge to write the Fearless Girls workshop in the first place. It changed everything, so I owe you (figuratively speaking, of course. . . you're not getting a cut of the royalties or nuffink).

The team at Wiley, for holding my hand so fastidiously through the process of writing my first book. You have the patience of saints, the whole lovely lot of you.

And then there's my co-author, Dr C.

You, sir, are a total lej. It goes without saying that this book wouldn't be in existence without you. Y'know that thing you do where you make people believe they can do anything? Yeah. Keep doing that. It's an epic quality. 'Thanks' doesn't even begin to cover it. But until they invent bigger words, it'll just have to do.

About the Authors

Suzie Lavington

My search for the secret to deep-down confidence was born out of the simple fact that in my teens and twenties, I had none. And when you're trying to make a living as an actor, that's far from ideal.

Sick of missing out on a bazillion opportunities thanks to my nerves and anxiety, I set out on a path to discover the cause of those feelings. . . and to kick them into touch once and for all.

Every single gem I uncovered on that little quest has been poured into this book (along with many more from the bonkersly brilliant Dr Cope). I'm beyond chuffed that it's been published ahead of my own girls, Amelie and Remy, reaching their teens. They are by far my proudest achievement, and if they can grow up in a world where self-esteem, confidence and kindness in girls are more abundant than they are today, then I can shuffle off this earth one *very* happy mama.

A Girl's Guide to Being Fearless may be my authorial debut but, hey, I'm fearless these days, so I don't mind saying that there's plenty more where this one came from. Watch this space.

A Girl's Guide to Being Fearless is available as a live and online workshop. Check it out at www.fearlessgirls.co.uk or on our Brilliant Schools website: www.brilliant.school

Drop me an email to suzie@artofbrilliance.co.uk
Twitter: @SuzieLavington
Insta: sincerely_suze
FB: artofbrilliance

Dr Andy Cope

Described by my mother as 'not even the best writer in this family', I have, nevertheless, managed to sell a million books worldwide. I am living proof that hard work trumps talent, every day of the week.

Weird fact, I'm also a doctor. Of sorts. I'm the UK's one and only Dr of Happiness, which pretty much makes me the total opposite of all the other doctors you've ever met. While they've been trained to work out what's wrong with you, I've been focused on what's right with you, what makes you come alive and how you can be at your best more often.

A quick bit of backstory – a couple of decades ago I decided that if I was going to change the world (which, with your help, I am) I would have to either give it a damn good go or die trying.

Honestly, right now, I'm not sure which will come first.

Either way, this little book is part of the revolution. I just Googled 'revolution' to check it's the right word and I'm not sure it is? Uprising, riot, overthrow, revolt, rebellion. . . that sounds a bit aggressive. I'm absolutely NOT asking you to grab a pitchfork and march to Parliament.

So to avoid any misunderstanding, I'm calling it a 'quiet revolution'. An uprising of wellbeing and mental health. It's a call to action to every person on the planet.

Quite simply, I want you to sign up to being your best self. No pitchforks required. No placards, no marching either. This revolution is so quiet that nobody will hear it because it takes place in your head.

But my goodness, they'll see it alright. Because once you sort things out between your ears, it shows in your behaviours, which ripple out into the community.

You become an example of what an awesome human being looks, sounds and feels like. That's what *Girl's Guide* has been about. Yes, dearest reader, I'm asking you to join a worldwide movement – a cunning plot to take over the world.

Welcome to global domination of the happiness kind.

Check me out at www.artofbrilliance.co.uk
Check out our Brilliant Schools website at www.brilliant.school
Drop me an email to andy@artofbrilliance.co.uk
Twitter @beingbrilliant
Insta artofbrilliance
FB artofbrilliance

Index

ALSO BY ANDY COPE

The Art of Being Brilliant: Transform Your Life by Doing What Works For You

Andy Cope and Andy Whittaker

9780857083715

Shine: Rediscovering Your Energy, Happiness and Purpose

Andy Cope and Gavin Oattes

9780857087652

Be Brilliant Every Day

Andy Cope and Andy Whittaker

9780857085009

Zest: How to Squeeze the Max out of Life

Andy Cope, Gavin Oattes and Will Hussey

9780857088000

The Little Book of Being Brilliant

Andy Cope

9780857087973

How to Be a Well Being: Unofficial Rules to Live Every Day

Andy Cope, Jim Pouliopoulos and Sanjeev Sandhu

9780857088673

············ FOR KIDS AND TEENAGERS ············

Diary of a Brilliant Kid: Top Secret Guide to Awesomeness

Andy Cope, Gavin Oattes and Will Hussey

9780857087867

The Art of Being a Brilliant Teenager

Andy Cope, Andy Whittaker, Darrell Woodman and Amy Bradley

9780857085788

CAPSTONE
A Wiley Brand